7·99

# RELIGIOUS EXPERIENCE

*access to religious studies*

# RELIGIOUS EXPERIENCE

*Peter Cole*

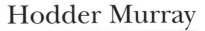
Hodder Murray
A MEMBER OF THE HODDER HEADLINE GROUP

The Publishers would like to thank the following for permission to reproduce copyright material:

**Photo credits**: AKG-images, page 61; © Bettmann/Corbis, page 5; © Mary Evans Picture Library 2005, pages 37, 47, 52; © Cenap Refik Ongan/Alamy, page 74; © Fredrik Renander/Alamy, page 19; Richard Swinburne, page 85.
**Acknowledgements:** Al-Islaah Publications for an extract used on pages 55–56; www.convertingtojudaism.com for an extract used on page 39.

Every effort has been made to trace all copyright holders, but if any have been inadvertently over-looked the Publishers will be pleased to make the necessary arrangements at the first opportunity.

Orders: please contact Bookpoint Ltd, 130 Milton Park, Abingdon, Oxon OX14 4SB. Telephone: (44) 01235 827720. Fax: (44) 01235 400454. Lines are open 9.00–6.00, Monday to Saturday, with a 24-hour message answering service. Visit our website at www.hoddereducation.co.uk

© Peter Cole 2005
First published in 2005 by
Hodder Murray, an imprint of Hodder Education,
a member of the Hodder Headline Group
338 Euston Road
London NW1 3BH

Impression number   10 9 8 7 6 5 4 3 2 1
Year                         2010 2009 2008 2007 2006 2005

Cover photo: *Fan Fire* (detail), 1997 (oil & glaze on gesso board) by Charlotte Johnstone (contemporary artist) Private Collection/Bridgeman Art Library Typeset in Baskerville and Gill and produced by Gray Publishing, Tunbridge Wells. Printed in Malta.

A catalogue record for this title is available from the British Library

ISBN-10: 0 340 84684 4
ISBN-13: 978 0340 84684 1

# Contents

# Preface

## To the student

Access books are written mainly for students studying for examinations at higher level, particularly GCE Advanced Subsidiary (AS) Level and Advanced (A) Level. A number of features have been included to assist students, such as the key words at the beginning of chapters and the material at the end of chapters.

To use these books most effectively, you should be aware of the following features:

- The contents list gives a breakdown of the sections in each chapter.
- The introductory chapter will set the scene for the material in the rest of the book.
- If you turn to the relevant chapters, you will find that they are broken down further into sub-headings and bullet-points. There are sometimes also Key Issues and Key Questions to focus your attention on important points.
- The key words at the beginning of each chapter are for easy reference and to help you become more familiar with the technical language of the subject. The key words that are defined are highlighted in bold in the main body of the text.
- There is also a section at the end of chapters on answering questions. This section includes a typical exam question with some specific advice on how to answer it. Do tackle the question, planning your answer and writing it in full.
- Throughout the book there are various thought-provoking questions that are taken up again in the 'Answering questions' section, providing some additional material.

## General advice on answering essay questions

Structured questions will tell you what to include. The following advice is for those questions that leave it to you to work out what should be included:

- The most important thing is to read the question carefully and work out what it really means. Make sure you understand all the words in the question (you may need to check some of them in the dictionary or look up technical terms in the key-word lists in the book).

- Gather the relevant information for answering the question. You will probably not need everything you know on the topic. Keep to what the question is asking.
- It is useful to have in your mind a quick checklist when doing exam essays. A possible checklist could include the following:

  ✓ Has the answer focused clearly on the issue in question?

  ✓ Does the answer relate back to the question?

  ✓ Does the answer show evidence of one year (or two years) of study (for example, by the correct use of technical terms and reference to named scholars)?

  Ask yourself:

  ✓ 'What does this fact illustrate?'

  ✓ 'Have I already illustrated that point?'

  ✓ 'Have I explained the relevance of this material to the slant of the question?'

  ✓ 'Does this add anything new to the argument?'

  ✓ 'Can I express it in a more concise way?'

# 1 Introduction

## 1 A fundamental question

> I heard nothing, yet it was as if I were surrounded by a golden light and as if I only had to reach out my hand to touch God himself who was surrounding me with his compassion. [183]

> I have a growing sense of reality, and personal identity, which comes from being united to something more powerful than myself, something that is helping me to be what I want to be. [843]

These two claims to some sort of religious experience are amongst the hundreds recorded by the Alister Hardy Trust on their website (*www.alisterhardytrust.org.uk*). Such experiences seem to be universal and seem to have occurred throughout time. What this book will do is not just discuss the sheer variety of such claimed experiences and the different attempts to classify them so they can be more easily discussed, but also raise a more fundamental question about the nature of religious experience.

The very understanding of what is meant by 'religious' is undergoing change. The growth of interest in '**New Age**' and **Paganism** are but two diverse elements among the many that are a feature of the early twenty-first century ideas. Such diversity focuses less on a theistic understanding of religion so that some would claim that 'God' has been removed from religion.

Chapter 2 examines this question by looking at the extent and variety of religious experiences. It also discusses the various attempts to group these experiences, by scholars (such as Richard Swinburne, William Stace and Caroline Franks Davis).

## 2 William James

Without doubt the classic book on religious experience is William James' *The Varieties of Religious Experience*, written in 1902. Born in 1842, he was the brother of the great novelist Henry James. William James' first book, *Principles of Psychology* (1890), established him as one of the most influential thinkers of his time. The work was instrumental in removing psychology from its traditional place as a branch of philosophy and establishing it among the laboratory sciences based on experimental method. This approach influenced his understanding of religious experience and his classic book on religious experience is a psychological account of religious and mystical experiences.

William James' classifications of religious experience have dominated and still remain the widely accepted framework over 100 years later.

Chapters 3–6 examine the key features of **mysticism**, conversion, visions and revelatory experiences.

## 3 Recent developments

One area that has proved to be of general interest is that of **near-death experience**, a term coined by Raymond Moody in his best-selling book *Life after Life* (1975). Moody happened to hear a couple of accounts of this phenomenon and this prompted him to start to investigate further; before long he had amassed a collection of some 150 experiences. Attempts were also made to find natural explanations that might account for this; recent developments in psychology and **physiology** have contributed to the debate. In the early 1970s, chemicals called endorphins were discovered and some saw in these the cause of the near-death vision as endorphins block some of the effects of trauma and shock. Research on genes and temporal lobes and the improved understanding of mental illness have all added to the debate about the nature of religious experiences.

Chapter 7 examines near-death experiences, while Chapter 8 considers some of the common triggers of religious experiences. The validity of religious experiences, including whether they are an argument for the existence of God, is debated in Chapters 9 and 10.

## 4 Are religious experiences important?

The religious experiences people have are important because they claim that these experiences are based on an objective reality (i.e. God/spirit/another world) and so may provide us with information about a possible spiritual realm. In other words they may inform us of the existence or otherwise of this other possible realm.

If the experiences either are false or can be explained without resorting to the hypothesis of a spiritual realm, then they do not give us information that leads us to believe in the existence of such a realm. If the experiences can be shown to be valid and can only be explained by the hypothesis of a spiritual realm, then they will have changed, or possibly confirmed, our views about the ultimate nature of reality. Whatever the truth behind these claimed experiences, they are undoubtedly taken very seriously by a number of people and have the effect of not only changing people's perception of the nature of reality but acting powerfully to change a whole range of areas of behaviour and ideas.

Religious experience has changed some people's lives very suddenly and dramatically. Would Mother Teresa have behaved in the way that she did without some sort of religious experience?

Chapter 11 examines the role and influence of religious experiences.

# 2 The Extent of Religious Experiences

## 1 Introduction

If you were to stand outside a shopping centre and ask people whether they had ever had a religious experience, what percentage do you think would answer positively? 5%? 10%? More?

Would you be surprised to find that roughly one-third of adults in Britain, the USA and Australia claimed to have had such experiences? In fact that is what researcher David Hay concluded (*Religious Experience Today*, 1990). He based his conclusions on various national surveys including the Religious Experience Research Centre national survey.

A similar survey in the United States asked 'Have you ever felt as though you were close to a powerful spiritual force that seemed to lift you out of yourself?'

Further research on prayer revealed that in Britain over 40% claim to pray daily, while in the USA it was over 60% (Poloma and Gallup, *The Varieties of Prayer: A Survey Report*, 1991).

A more recent survey was undertaken in Finland by the Church Research Centre. Here, a total of 2500 Finns were interviewed in early 2001. It was found that one in three Finns (37%) said that they had received help from God at some point in their life and one in four Finns believed that they had received an answer to prayer.

## 2 Religious experience research

Probably the first major research into religious experience was by William James (1842–1910). His book, *The Varieties of Religious Experience* (1902), has remained a classic. The book is based on a series of 20 public lectures that he was invited to deliver at Edinburgh University on the theme of natural religion. He analysed religious experiences, mostly from literary sources of people's experiences 'in their solitude'. Often he used famous examples of religious visions. Thus, the sample did not represent the experiences of the general population. Indeed he declared that he would exclude from consideration the 'ordinary religious believer, who follows the conventional observances of his country'. It was left to later research to consider wider experiences from a more diverse population. Clearly there are problems in collecting such data. Can you think of some of these difficulties?

In 1969 Alister Hardy set up the Religious Experience Research Unit (RERU) in Oxford with the object of examining the extent and nature of the religious experiences of people in Britain. It was later called the Alister Hardy Research Centre and moved to the University of Wales, Lampeter in 2000. Hardy advertised in British papers and

William James (1842–1910)

magazines, inviting people to write to him, replying to the following question:

> Have you ever been aware of or influenced by a presence or power, whether you call it God or not, which is different from your everyday self?

This resulted in about 7000 replies of which 3000 were analysed and written up in his book *The Spiritual Nature of Man* (1979). Later, information was collected by survey rather than relying on people writing in.

## 3 The variety of religious experiences

**KEY ISSUE** What soon became obvious was the sheer breadth and variety of such experiences. People included in their replies to researchers accounts of paranormal experiences as well as the more traditional religious experience. These included claims of people's visions of the Virgin Mary and of angels. The Charismatic Movement has also drawn attention to such experiences as '**speaking in tongues**', 'prophecy' and 'words of knowledge'.

As well as these, some accounts of negative experiences have recently been studied by Jakobsen (*Negative Religious Experiences*, 1999) using the collection of material set up by Sir Alister Hardy. The experience of evil continues to be a reported experience, with Poloma (*The Toronto Report*, 1996) reporting that 55% of a **Toronto Blessing** group thought they had been 'delivered from Satan's hold'.

Since William James' book, we have become more aware of the variety of religious experiences, and there has been a growth of interest in the paranormal and near-death experiences. The religious significance of psychic experiences has been questioned. In the survey carried out by Hay and Heald in 1987 (*Religion is good for you*, *New Society*, 17 March) it was found that of the 18% who reported awareness of the presence of someone who had died, only 35% of them thought this was religious.

We have also become increasingly aware of a wide variety of religions, including not just the main world religions but the New Religious Movements as well as New Age and Paganism, such as **Wicca** and **Druidry**. Dr Harvey (*Religious Experience in Contemporary Society*, 1997) drew attention to this diversity and in particular the new perspective that Paganism and **animism** have contributed to the study, and concluded that

> There is no single thing that can be bottled and neatly labelled as 'religious experience'. What happens in an Anglican **eucharist** is not the same as in an **Hasidic Seder** ... the range of experiences which people label 'spiritual' vary far more than some commentators have allowed.

## 4 Differences between 'religious' and 'ordinary' experiences

The Alister Hardy collection, according to David Hay, shows clear evidence of claims of experiences that were quite different from other types of experience people had. The religious experience

> … usually induces in the person concerned a conviction that the everyday world is not the whole of reality; there is another dimension to life … awareness of its presence affects the person's view of the world, it alters behaviour and changes attitudes.
>
> *(Inner Space, 1987)*

Among the differences between 'religious' and 'ordinary' experiences are:

- Religious experiences are wholly other from what is customary and usual.
- God is experienced as opposed to everyday physical objects. A person experiences a spiritual change that clearly has a religious dimension (e.g. a person has a new desire to pray and read the Bible).
- It is not usual to be able to describe the religious experience adequately because it is so unlike any thing else. We do not have suitable words in our vocabulary.
- The religious experience is not universal to human beings (i.e. we do not all have religious experiences but we all experience a tree, etc.).
- Human beings basically use the same conceptual scheme when they describe an ordinary experience. Regardless of culture we all describe a tree in the same way. However with religious experience, though the feeling may be similar (e.g. awe), the object is different (e.g. Jesus, Shiva, Muhammad). In other words, religious experiences have different interpretations in different cultures.
- Often a religious experience is a subjective experience, whereas an ordinary experience is objective (i.e. the religious experience often has its source within the mind, while ordinary experiences have their source external to the mind and so actually exist).
- Religious experience cannot generally be checked, whereas an ordinary experience is open to checking (e.g. can be seen by others).
- Religious experience gives insight into the unseen whereas the ordinary gives no insight into other realms.
- God cannot be experienced unless He allows it. In contrast, an ordinary experience may be experienced by anyone in the right place at the right time with the requisite sense organs.

## 5 What is the nature of a religious experience?

So, what is the nature of these experiences that seem for many to point them to belief in God or some sense of being part of some ultimate reality? One immediate problem is that they tend to be subjective. That means that the subject has privileged access to the experience, i.e. I can't experience your experience since it is happening inside your mind to which I have no access. The nearest I can come to it I suppose is to listen to you describing it. But here is another problem. You seem to be having a problem describing it. Consider this example cited by William James (*The Varieties of Religious Experience*, 1902).

> All at once I ... felt the presence of God ... I tell of the thing just as I was conscious of it – as if his goodness and his power were penetrating me altogether. The more I seek words to express this intimate intercourse, the more I feel the impossibility of describing the thing. At bottom the expression most apt to render what I felt is this: God was present, though invisible; he fell under not one of my senses, yet my consciousness perceived him.

### a) Can religious experiences be classified into groups?

Given the wide variety of experiences, it is not surprising that people have attempted to find some way of grouping them or trying to collate features that are common. For instance, a basic grouping is of experiences where there is contact with a **transcendent** being. The features in this case are awe and dependence. This is in contrast to those experiences that feature a more inward and **immanent** awareness.

Swinburne (*The Existence of God*, 1979) identifies five types of religious experience in which a person seems to perceive God classified according to how the experiences come about:

- Experiencing a perfectly normal non-religious object or event, e.g. a night sky. The night sky is not God, but God is encountered through it. The object or event is seen as the handiwork of God, a sign from God, an address by God or that which points to God.
- Experiencing a very unusual public object, e.g. the resurrection appearances of Jesus or the appearance of the Virgin Mary at Lourdes.
- Experiencing private sensations that are describable by normal vocabulary, e.g. Joseph's dream of the angel.
- Experiencing private sensations that are not describable by normal vocabulary, e.g. a mystical experience such as those of St Teresa of Avila (see page 21).
- Non-sensory experience. They would be unable to refer to anything in particular that made it seem they were experiencing God. 'It just did!'

The first two are public events, as in theory other people present could have seen what was happening and experienced God through the event. The last three are private.

Caroline Franks Davis has a different six-fold listing in Chapter 2 of her book *The Evidential Force of Religious Experience* (1989):

- *Interpretive experiences* – an event that has no specifically religious characteristics is attributed to a divine source by a person with prior religious beliefs, e.g. an answer to prayer.
- *Quasi-sensory experiences* – the primary element is a physical sensation, such as a vision or hearing a voice.
- *Revelatory experiences* – the 'enlightenment' experience in which their religious content make them a religious experience.
- *Regenerative experiences* – a conversion experience or an experience that renews the person's faith.
- *Numinous experiences* – an experience of God's unapproachable holiness.
- *Mystical experiences* – the sense of apprehending ultimate reality or a oneness with God.

These are the main categories that will be considered in the following chapters. The categories are not mutually exclusive, since an experience may exhibit characteristics of several categories. Others have drawn together various features in order to try to group religious experiences. For example:

- Awareness is experiential rather than thinking or reasoning (e.g. Joan of Arc's visions were something that she claimed to experience rather than reason).
- Experience is direct, rather than awareness through something else (e.g. the claim of some mystics that they have 'become one with God'). However there are also those that are not direct, such as those that claim to experience God through nature. An example from Islam could be the experience of the awareness of God in the observation of creation. The Qur'an describes the phenomena of nature as 'signs' of God: 'Verily in the heavens and the earth, are Signs for those who believe.' (45:3)
- The experience is often lacking sensory content. You don't actually see God, etc.

## b) Is there a common core?

So do some features commonly occur in most religious experiences? Is there a common core? Probably the most cited list is that from Walter Stace (*Mysticism and Philosophy*, 1960). His eight-fold list of features of religious experiences is:

- The unifying vision, expressed abstractly by the formula 'All is One'. All things are one, part of a whole.

- Timelessness and spacelessness.
- Sense of reality, not subjective but a valid source of knowledge.
- Blessedness, joy, peace and happiness.
- Feeling that what is apprehended is holy, or sacred, or divine. This is the quality that gives rise to the interpretation of the experience as being an experience of 'God'.
- Sense of the presence of paradox and logic defied.
- **Ineffability**, cannot be described in words.
- Loss of the sense of self.

Many feel Stace only concentrated on the immanent type of accounts and ignored accounts involving a transcendent experience – a being outside of oneself evoking awe and dependence. There is also no mention of an enhanced feeling of love and concern and unity with others, or of any sensory aspects such as visions or light, which are often reported. Therefore possibly a better, fuller list is given by Greeley, based on his national US sample of 1467 people (*Sociology of the Paranormal*, 1975).

| Descriptor | % |
| --- | --- |
| A feeling of deep and profound peace | 55% |
| A certainty that all things would work out for the good | 48% |
| A sense of my own need to contribute to others | 43% |
| A conviction that love is the centre of everything | 43% |
| A sense of joy and laughter | 43% |
| An experience of great emotional intensity | 38% |
| A great increase in my understanding and knowledge | 32% |
| A sense of the unity of everything and my own part in it | 29% |
| A sense of a new life and living in a new world | 27% |
| A confidence in my own personal survival | 27% |
| A feeling that I couldn't possibly describe what was happening to me | 26% |
| A sense that all the universe is alive | 25% |
| The sense that my personality has been taken over by something much more powerful than I am | 24% |
| A sensation of warmth or fire | 22% |
| A sense of being alone | 19% |
| A loss of concern about worldly problems | 19% |
| A sense that I am being bathed in light | 14% |
| A sense of desolation | 8% |

## c) Can religious experience be defined?

Philosophy is notorious for asking awkward questions about things that most consider obvious and straightforward! Not surprisingly then, philosophers have raised questions about the meaning of the words 'religious' and 'experience'.

## i) Religious

Anthony Thiselton (*A Concise Encyclopedia of the Philosophy of Religion*, 2002) highlights three factors in post-modern thought that make defining 'religion' and 'religious' a problem. First, there is the awareness of diversity and pluralism and a growing reluctance to generalise. The word 'religious' can mean almost anything, but because of this it can mean very little. Secondly, there is the recognition that our knowledge and understanding are conditioned by our own intellectual background. They are not value-neutral. Thiselton cites Wittgenstein's criticisms of Frazer:

> Wittgenstein criticised Frazer's *The Golden Bough* for offering 'explanations' of the beliefs and practices of other cultures and other religions as if these were practised by men who think in a similar way to himself. Frazer too readily 'explained' them in such a way as to make them seem 'stupidities', because he abstracted them from the life-context that made them intelligible. (pages 256–257)

Finally, he notes that the post-modern view of religions has viewed them as serving vested interests of social power, and so has viewed them sociologically or ideologically, rather than theologically. In other words, we take the 'God' out of them.

## ii) Experience

One meaning of 'to experience' is 'to participate in' or 'to live through'. We might talk about having experience with cars. This poses no problem as the event is in the public sphere, i.e. other people can see you working on a car. The other meaning of 'experience' however is more problematic. It is to 'directly perceive', 'be aware of' or 'be conscious of'. In this case the experience is subjective and private. It is some inner process that others cannot see. Therefore no-one can refute my claim that I am experiencing something, even if the source is disputed. If I claim to hear the voice of God, there is no way of either verifying or falsifying that claim. The claimed source of the experience is beyond our powers of investigation.

Steven Katz argues that there is no experience that is unmediated by concepts and beliefs. All experience is processed through the beliefs, learned categories and conceptual frameworks of the experiencer, i.e. religious belief conditions religious experience so that persons in different religious traditions actually experience differently. There is not one religious experience but many.

## iii) Some definitions

Despite all these problems, we still need some sort of working definition for the term 'religious experience'. One definition could be 'an experience that has religious insight'. This insight is usually the unseen dimensions of existence and it requires that God or Ultimate Reality be the object of the experience.

Alister Hardy (*The Spiritual Nature of Man*, 1979) defined religious experience as:

> The experience ... usually induces in the person concerned a conviction that the everyday world is not the whole of reality; there is another dimension to life ... it alters behaviour and changes attitudes ... [and] may be seen by an individual as life-enhancing, or he may recognise it as a special force which gives him added confidence or courage. As a result of their experiences many are led to prayer and religion.

Ninian Smart (*The Religious Experience of Mankind*, 1969) defines it in a similar way:

> A religious experience involves some kind of 'perception' of the invisible world, or involves a perception that some visible person or thing is a manifestation of the invisible world.

Other definitions focus on an experience as an event that one lives through and of which one is conscious or aware. To be a religious experience, that which is experienced is either some supernatural being/God, or a being related to God, e.g. Virgin Mary, or some indescribable Ultimate Reality. Hence religious experiences can be **theistic** (where God is the source and content of the experience) or **monistic** (where inner being/consciousness is experienced), as monism is the view that all reality is a unity or single substance.

Of course many people with mental illness or who are under the influence of drugs claim experiences. Those who argue that the source has to be valid would refuse to accept these as genuine, while others may include them on the grounds that they result in some spiritual insight or break down the barrier between the conscious and the unconscious mind. Indeed one definition of a religious experience is any experience that is given a religious interpretation.

## Answering questions on Chapter 2

By the end of this chapter you should appreciate the wide variety of religious experiences that have been reported and know their core key features. You should also know the key differences between ordinary and religious experiences, and be able to discuss the problems of defining the term 'religious experience'.

Did you manage to think of some problems connected with collecting data about religious experience? One problem is the lack of agreement as to what counts as a religious experience. Also the wide variety of experiences would make it difficult to handle unless there were some way to group them. This is an issue that is examined in Chapter 3.

Do you agree with the list of differences between ordinary and religious experiences? Can you add any more? Try considering the similarities rather than differences between ordinary and religious experiences. Maybe Swinburne's five types or Caroline Franks Davis' six-fold list will give you some ideas. What would you reply to someone who argued that if God is in all things then in one sense every 'ordinary' experience is a religious experience?

The sort of exam questions asked, based on this chapter, involve defining a religious experience, e.g. *Explain what is meant by religious experience*. Often candidates discuss types of religious experience rather than a general or overarching term. As a result they attempt to write all they know about every type of religious experience. Clearly what is required is an understanding that there is some controversy about what exactly a religious experience is. It is also important to illustrate with examples, highlighting **how** they illustrate the definition given.

These definitions do raise issues about validity. For instance, would you consider the claims of a schizophrenic to hear the voice of God a religious experience? Is it reasonable to distinguish between 'genuine' religious experiences and 'non-genuine'? Indeed is there a valid distinction? For a fuller discussion on this, see Chapters 9 and 10.

# 3 Mysticism

**KEY ISSUE** In Lecture 16 of *The Varieties of Religious Experience*, James argued that '… personal religious experience has its root and centre in mystical states of consciousness …'.

## 1 The meaning of 'mysticism'

The word 'mystical' is derived from the Greek root word 'mu', meaning to close or to hide. Strangely enough, it was the adjective 'mystical' that was originally used and the nouns mystic (a distinct kind of person) and mysticism (a distinct kind of experience) did not come into common use until the sixteenth and seventeenth centuries. The ancient Greeks used the term mystical in connection with the mystery religions where the initiated gained access to knowledge of divine things. However the initiated were not allowed to share this knowledge with the uninitiated. Hence the word is associated with people who have direct and intimate experiences of God.

Teasdall (*The Mystic Heart*, 1999) defines mysticism as 'direct, immediate experience of ultimate reality. For Christians, it is union and communion with God. For Buddhists, it is realization of enlightenment'. However it is by no means clear that, for instance, the Buddhist and the Christian mean the same thing by either unity or reality when they refer to an experience of unity with ultimate reality.

Bauerschmidt (*Why the Mystics Matter Now*, 2003) defines the term mystic as 'someone who has experienced an altered state of consciousness that has brought them to a new awareness of ultimate reality' (page 8), and William James (*The Varieties of Religious Experience*) says it is an ability to see truth in a special way.

# 2 The features of mysticism

> **KEY ISSUE** How can we identify a mystical experience?

According to James there are four marks that an experience should have in order to justify us calling it mystical:

- *Ineffability*: Mystical experiences are states of feelings so unlike anything else that it is not possible to impart or transfer them to others. No adequate account of the experience can be given in words. They defy expression. Phrases such as 'the dissolution of the personal ego' are empty phrases to those who have not experienced such things. Thus it follows that the experience must be immediate and direct, since it cannot be imparted to others. No one can make clear to another, who has never had a certain feeling, its quality or worth. James uses the analogy with music and says that it is like the need to have musical ears in order to know the value of a symphony. Without such a musical ear, we are likely to consider the musician absurd. See Chapter 11, pages 106–107 for further discussion on this topic.
- *Noetic quality*: Mystical states seem to be states of knowledge to those that experience them. They are states that allow insight into the depths of truth unobtainable by the intellect alone. They are illuminations, revelations full of importance and significance. They are universal and eternal truths. This feeling of insight or illumination is felt on an intuitive, non-rational level and has a tremendous force of certainty and reality.
- *Transiency*: Mystical states cannot be maintained for long periods of time. James claims that, except in rare cases, 30 minutes to two hours is the limit. Though these states are remembered, they are imperfectly recalled. Usually they leave the recipient with a profound sense of the importance of the experience.
- *Passivity*: Although a mystical state may be entered through meditation, etc., the characteristic state of consciousness is one of passivity or acceptance and openness. In such a state the mystic will feel as if he or she is taken over by a superior power.

Happold (*Mysticism: A Study and Anthology*, 1963) identified another three characteristics of the mystical experience:

- *Consciousness of the oneness of everything* – this seems to be a sense of cosmic oneness. The usual awareness of identity, or ego, fades away and the person becomes aware of being part of a dimension much greater than themselves. This unity can be either introvertive, where external sense impressions are left behind, or extrovertive, where the person reports that he feels a part of everything that is (e.g. objects, other people, nature or the universe) or, more simply, that 'all is one'. For some this is the defining feature that serves to mark them off from other kinds of experiences. Many experiences have been recorded that lack this central feature of the consciousness of the oneness yet possess other mystical characteristics.

- *Sense of timelessness* – the subject feels beyond past, present and future, and beyond ordinary three-dimensional space in a realm of eternity or infinity.
- *The understanding that the ego is not the real 'I'* – this seems to be a sense that there is an unchanging self that is immortal and that lies behind the usual experience of self.

Another study by Walter Pahnke (*Psychedelic Review*, 1971) was based on literature of spontaneous mystical experiences reported throughout world history from almost all cultures and religions. He identified similar features to James and Happold, though he did list five other characteristics:

- *Deeply felt positive mood* – this contains the elements of joy, blessedness, peace and love to an overwhelming degree of intensity, often accompanied by tears.
- *Sense of sacredness* – this is a non-rational, intuitive, hushed response of awe and wonder in the presence of inspiring reality. The main elements are awe, humility and reverence.
- *Paradoxicality* – this refers to the logical contradictions that become apparent if descriptions are carefully analysed. A person may realise that they are experiencing, for example, an 'identity of opposites', yet it seems to make sense at the time, and also afterwards.
- *Alleged ineffability* – (as opposed to James' ineffability) this means that the experience is felt to be beyond words, non-verbal and impossible to describe; yet most persons who insist on ineffability do in fact make elaborate attempts to communicate the experience, usually by means of imagery or metaphor. For further discussion on this see Chapter 11 (page 106).
- *Persisting positive changes in attitudes and behaviour* – these changes in attitude are towards self, others, life and the experience itself.

If you look back to Chapter 2 (page 9) you will see that the list of Walter Stace's common core features mirror very closely those listed above for mystical experiences.

> Now, four days after the experience itself, I continue to feel a deep sense of awe and reverence, being simultaneously intoxicated with an ecstatic joy. This euphoric feeling... includes elements of profound peace and steadfastness, surging like a spring from a depth of my being...
>
> [In the experience] ... , I transcended my usual level of consciousness and became aware of fantastic dimensions of being, all of which possessed a profound sense of reality.
>
> ... It would seem more accurate to say that I existed 'in' these dimensions of being as I had not only transcended my ego, but also the dichotomy between subject and object.

It is meaningful to say that I ceased to exist, becoming immersed in the ground of Being, in Brahman, in God, in 'Nothingness', in Ultimate Reality or in some similar religious symbol for Oneness ...

The feelings I experienced could best be described as cosmic tenderness, infinite love, penetrating peace, eternal blessing and unconditional acceptance on one hand, and on the other, as unspeakable awe, overflowing joy, primeval humility, inexpressible gratitude and boundless devotion. Yet all of these words are hopelessly inadequate and can do little more than meekly point towards the genuine, inexpressible feelings actually experienced.

It is misleading even to use the words 'I experienced', since during the peak of the experience (which must have lasted at least an hour) there was no duality between myself and what I experienced. Rather, I was these feelings, or ceased to be in them and felt no loss at the cessation. This was especially evident when, after having reached the mystic peak, a recording of Bach's 'Fantasia and Fugue in G Minor' was played. At this time it seemed as though I was not M. R. listening to a recording, but paradoxically was the music itself. Especially at one climax in the Fantasia, the 'love' I was experiencing became so overwhelming as to become unbearable or even painful. The tears I shed at this moment were in no sense those of fear, but ones of uncontainable joy.

... During the height of the experience, I had no consciousness of time or space in the ordinary sense. I felt as though I was beyond seconds, minutes, hours, and also beyond past, present, and future. In religious language, I was in eternity.

... Let me affirm that even with my acquaintance with mystic literature of both east and west, coupled with the profound appreciation of natural and artistic beauty I have always enjoyed, I know I could never have understood this experience, had I not lived it myself. The dimensions of being I entered surpassed the wildest fantasies of my imagination and, as I have said, leave me with a profound sense of awe.... In no sense have I an urge to formulate philosophical or theological dogmas about my experience. Only my silence can retain its purity and genuineness.

(The psychedelic mystical experience in the human encounter with death. *Psychedelic Review*, Number 11, 1971)

Can you identify which features of a mystic experience were **not** contained in this account?

Not all mystical experiences are necessarily religious. As we saw in Chapter 2 (page 11), much depends upon how religion is defined. If you make the concept of a 'personal God' central to the definition of religion, many forms of mystical experience could not be considered to be religious. The phenomena of mystical experience may occur outside the framework of any formal religion with no reference to an articulated theology.

The problem is by-passed rather than solved by broadening the definition of religion to include any experience that would qualify as mystical by our criteria. Paul Tillich, for example, considers an experience religious when it gives ultimate meaning, structure and direction to human experience, or when one is concerned 'ultimately' (Tillich, 1951). An experience that elicits from the experiencer, a centred response from the core of his being, is another definition used of religious experience. This could then include such feelings as awe, belief and will. Whether or not mystical experience is religious depends upon one's definition of religion.

## 3 Examples of mysticism

### a) Hindu mysticism

Hinduism has perhaps the oldest tradition of mysticism. The self (atman) in a person is identified with the supreme self (Brahman) of the universe. The apparent separateness and individuality of beings and events are held to be an illusion (maya). This illusion can be dispelled through the realisation of the essential oneness of atman and Brahman. Then a mystical state of liberation (moksha) is attained. The Hindu philosophy of Yoga is a discipline to experience union with the divine self.

> When his soul is in peace he is in peace, and then his soul is in God ... The Yogi who, lord of his mind, ever prays in this harmony of soul, attains the peace of Nirvana, the peace supreme that is in me ... Thus joy supreme comes to the Yogi whose heart is still, whose passions are peace, who is pure from sin, who is one with Brahman, with God.
>
> (*Bhagavad Gita* 6:7,15,27)

Another attempt to describe this attained state is in Brhadaranyaka Upanishad IV,3.

> Like a man who is enveloped in sexual embrace ... is not aware of anything at all that is outside or inside ... once he has merged with the self that is wisdom, he knows nothing at all what is outside or inside. That now is his form in which his desires are fulfilled, his passions are his own self, his cravings cease, and in which all unhappiness has come to an end.

Another example from the Brhadaranyaka Upanishad II,2 describes the merging of the self with the Absolute:

> ... as a lump of salt cast in water would dissolve right into the water .... Arising out of these elements (bhuta), into them also one vanishes away ...

### b) Buddhist mysticism

Meditation is a key aspect of practice in most schools of Buddhism. There is a range of different techniques and approaches, from quietly concentrating on your breathing to reciting mantras. The technique of mental concentration is called samatha, and its aim is to discover the real nature of the body and mind by overcoming attachments. A mantra is a short phrase and some believe that reciting the phrase in itself is sufficient to reveal enlightenment.

Zen Buddhism has a particular understanding of the idea of the dissolution of individuality, which contrasts markedly with that of Hinduism.

> The individual shell in which my personality is so solidly encased explodes at the moment of satori. ... my individuality ... melts away into something indescribable, something which is of quite a different order from what I am accustomed to.
>
> (cited by Franks Davis, *The Evidential Force of Religious Experience*, 1989, page 57)

The key Zen practice is 'zazen'. This involves sitting in one of several available positions and meditating so that you become fully in touch with the true nature of reality. In Zen Buddhism, enlightenment is generally thought of as being sudden.

Buddhist meditations

## c) Jewish mysticism

Mysticism and mystical experiences have been a part of Judaism since the earliest days and the Torah contains many stories of mystical experiences such as visitations by angels. Just as there is a written Torah, there was also an oral Torah that gave the inner meaning of the Torah. It is this oral Torah that is supposedly handed down by word of mouth (although since the twelfth century it has been committed to writing) that constitutes the **Kabbalah**. Hence the Kabbalah is the mystical branch of Judaism, just as **Sufism** is the mystical tradition within Islam.

Originally the two primary subjects of mystical thought were ma'aseh bereishit (the work of creation) and ma'aseh merkavah (the work of the chariot [of Ezekiel's vision]) (see below).

In the middle ages, many of these mystical teachings were committed to writing in books like the Zohar. Many of these writings were asserted to be secret ancient writings or compilations of secret ancient writings.

There are elements of kabbalah in the Bible, for example, in the opening chapter of Ezekiel, where the prophet describes his experience of the divine: '… the heavens were opened and I saw visions of God. … I looked and I saw a windstorm coming out of the north – an immense cloud with flashing lightning and surrounded by a brilliant light' (Ezekiel 1:1,4). The prophet then describes a divine chariot and the throne of God.

The early modern period witnessed growing dissatisfaction with rabbinic leadership, and a number of Jews began to seek individual salvation through religious pietism. This movement, called the Hasidic movement, emphasised good deeds and piety through joy of worship. Its founder, Rabbi Israel Baal Shem Tov, gave an account of a mystical experience he had:

> On the day of the New Year of the year 5507 (1746 AD) I engaged in an ascent of the soul, as you know I do, and I saw wondrous things in that vision that I had never before seen since the day I had attained to maturity. That which I saw and learned in my ascent it is impossible to describe or to relate even from mouth to mouth …'.
>
> (*Jewish and Christian Mysticism*, 1994)

## d) Christian mysticism

Christian mysticism is often described as 'union with God'. Appeal is made to the Bible for support for such a union with God. The doctrine of incarnation (God becoming flesh) is central to this idea. So are such passages as John 15 with the imagery of Jesus as the vine and his followers as the branches, or John 17:20–23 with Jesus' prayer for union. The Song of Solomon in the Old Testament also contains such ideas. The Song of Solomon consists of a series of poems on the theme of love between man and woman, which many interpret allegorically as Christ's love for his bride the Church.

The term generally used until the fourteenth and fifteenth centuries, to describe mystical experiences, was '**contemplation**'. Although prayer can be considered 'contemplation', it has been usual to reserve 'mystic' to refer to the extraordinary experience involving the work of God's grace taking over the person.

Some criticise mystical union, claiming that it tends towards pantheism, with the individual identity of the soul being lost and absorbed into God. Others defend it by saying that the soul is not losing itself but finding its true identity.

## i) Particular mystics

An example of mysticism from a Christian mystic is from St Catherine of Genoa (1447–1510)

> O that I could tell you what the heart feels, how it burns and is consumed inwardly! Only, I find no words to express it. I can but say: Might but one little drop of what I feel fall into Hell, Hell would be transformed into a Paradise.

One of the most often quoted Christian mystics is St Teresa of Avila (1515–1582). Teresa wrote about her mystical experiences and the ineffable characteristic is prevalent, e.g. in *The Collected Work of St Teresa of Avila* (1987):

> the soul is fully awake as regards God, but wholly asleep as regards things of this world.
>
> God establishes himself in the interior of this soul in such a way that, when I return to myself, it is wholly impossible for me to doubt that I have been in God, and God in me.
>
> It was granted me to perceive in one instant how all things are seen and contained in God. I did not perceive them in their proper form, and nevertheless the view I had of them was of a sovereign clearness, and has remained vividly impressed upon my soul. ... This view was so subtle and delicate that the understanding cannot grasp it.

Teresa's most famous book *The Interior Castle* describes a person's soul as a multi-chamber castle. Going deeper and deeper into your soul and facing your own fears, self-interest, ego and temptations gradually leads you to a deeper relationship with God. At the very central chamber the soul is at complete peace and complete union with God.

Teresa's contemporary, John of the Cross (1542–1591), refers to a state in which 'all the movements and operations which the soul had aforetime ... are now in this union changed into movements of God' (*Living Flame of Love*, 1962).

## ii) Recent Neo-Pentecostal phenomena

Two recent phenomena that have stirred controversy within the Christian faith are 'being slain in the Spirit' ('resting in the Spirit') and the 'Toronto Blessing'. Both have their roots in the **Charismatic** Movement, which, in turn, emerged from **Pentecostalism**. The first is said to occur when a believer is overtaken by the power of the Holy Spirit. The person loses all motor control over their body and falls backwards to the ground. The context for it is often a revival meeting or a prayer-and-praise service. It is often brought on when the preacher or designated assistant comes directly to a person and lays hands on them or speaks a prayer over them.

The 'Toronto Blessing' is a movement that began in 1994 at the Toronto Airport Vineyard Church but has since spread around the world. The phenomena include people weeping uncontrollably, others laughing hysterically, some toppling over or crumpling silently to the floor, while others jerk and twitch, acting as if they were drunk, doubling over with abdominal spasms, roaring like a lion or barking like a dog.

Many claim these phenomena are without Biblical support and either that people become hysterical (with excitement) and pass out, or that it is some sort of mesmerising (hypnosis) because people: (a) expect to feel this and (b) the preacher is suggesting this is going to happen.

Other Charismatic phenomena such as 'speaking in tongues' and 'words of knowledge' will be discussed in Chapters 5 and 6.

## e) Muslim mysticism

Islamic doctrine rejects the idea of Allah's literal presence within matter, though the Qur'an does describe creation as a 'sign' of Allah (50:20). However, a more mystical concept is implied by Sara Qaf 50:13 '(Allah is) … nearer to man than his jugular vein'. Zaehner (*Hindu and Muslim Mysticism*, 1994) quotes from an utterance attributed to Abu Yazid:

Adorn me with Thy Unity,
Clothe me with The Selfhood,
And raise me up to Thy Oneness,
So that when Thy creatures see me
They will say we have seen Thee
And thou art That.

(page 94)

Sufism is the inner, mystical dimension of Islam. One person who made Sufism more acceptable within Islam was Al-Ghazali (1059–1111 CE). He emphasised the personal, inner religious faith that should accompany the external practices of the religion.

However, many Muslims and non-Muslims believe that Sufism is outside the sphere of Islam. All Muslims believe that they are on the pathway to God and will become close to Allah in Paradise – after death and the 'Final Judgment'. Sufis believe that it is possible to become close to God and to experience this closeness in this life now.

'In the Presence', says the Sufi mystic [Shabistari], ' "I" and "thou" have ceased to exist, they have become one; the Quest and the Way and the Seeker are one' (*The Mystics of Islam*, 1914).

# 4 Types of mysticism

> **KEY ISSUE** There has been much debate about whether the mystical experiences reported in different cultures and traditions are basically of the same type, or whether there are significantly different types or even whether it is possible to classify them at all.

## a) They are all one and the same

This view regards mysticism as a universal phenomenon of the human spirit experiencing communion with God (or absorption into the Absolute). It is essentially the same whether Christian or Jewish, Hindu or Buddhist. The tradition or culture is irrelevant. To account for some of the apparent differences between the accounts of the experiences, a difference is made between the experience and its interpretation. They all experience the same thing but they interpret their experiences differently, in accordance with their varying cultures and religious traditions.

## b) There are a few types that cut cultural barriers

Those who support this view do not all agree as to what these types are. For instance Walter Stace (*Mysticism and Philosophy*, 1960) identifies two basic types of mystical experience. Both are apprehensions of the One, but they are reached in different ways:

- *Extrovertive* – looks outwardly and through the physical senses to the external world. The external world is transfigured in such a way that the Unity shines through them.
- *Introvertive* – turns inwardly, introspectively, losing identity as a separate individual and merging into the divine Unity. For instance the Mandukya (Upanishads) says that it is 'beyond the senses, beyond the understanding, beyond all expression … . It is the pure unitary consciousness, wherein awareness of the world and of multiplicity is completely obliterated. … It is the Self'.

Stace argues that this introvertive experience is the purest as it is non-sensuous and non-intellectual, where the empirical conscious-ness has been suppressed. It is cross-cultural in that the essence of this experience is undifferentiated unity, though he sees this inter-preted differently in each culture and religion.

Zaehner (*Mysticism: Sacred and Profane*, 1957) distinguishes three types:

*   *Nature* – the experience of oneness with nature. For example 'I felt myself one with the grass, the trees, birds, everything in Nature'. The poet Wordsworth often reflects this view in his writings (e.g. *Tintern Abbey*).
*   *Monistic* – the experience of my own spirit as the Absolute, the identity of Atman and Brahman. This is found more in Eastern traditions, e.g. Taoism, which seeks unity with Tao, the ineffable way.
*   *Theistic* – union or communion with a personal Lord or Creator. This is non-absorptive and more related to Western traditions with monotheistic faiths.

Ninian Smart (*Philosophers and Religious Truth*, 1964) rejects the dif-ference between monistic and theistic, seeing this as interpretation rather than a different experience. However he does distinguish between the experience of the numinous and the mystical. For dis-cussion about the numinous see Section 5 below.

### c) It is impossible to classify them

Scholars like Steven Katz argue that there is no such thing as a pure or unmediated experience. The experience itself is shaped both by the concepts that the mystic brings to it and by the form in which it is reported. Hence Christians experience union with Christ; Hindus experience identification with Atman; Buddhists experience 'emptiness'.

## 5 Mysticism and the numinous

Ninian Smart (*Philosophers and Religious Truth*, 1964) agreed that mystic experiences could be classified into types but he distinguished between the experience of the numinous (the prophetic experience) and the mystical experience. Among the differences he noted were:

*   The **numinous** experience always involves an awareness of how different the experiencer is to the Deity. In mysticism there is an emphasis on union.
*   The numinous experience involves a sense of dependency on something external, whereas the mystic experience focuses on the internal.

- The numinous experience usually happens suddenly and unexpectedly, whereas in mysticism there is often preparation.

The term 'numinous' was coined by Rudolf Otto (1869–1937) in his book *The Idea of the Holy* (1917). He argued that there is one common factor to all religious experience, independent of the cultural background, and it is this experience that he identifies as the 'numinous'.

The deepest and most fundamental element in all strong and sincerely felt religious emotion.

The word comes from the Latin 'numen', meaning divinity. For Otto, religious experience is about a feeling. In particular, experience of the holy. However because the word 'holy' had so many associations, he used 'numen'. It is something that is 'wholly other' than the natural world, and beyond apprehension and comprehension. He analysed this type of experience in terms of the Latin phrase *mysterium tremendum et fascinans*:

Beyond our apprehension and comprehension, not only because our knowledge has certain irremovable limits, but because in it we come upon something inherently 'wholly other', whose kind and character are incommensurable with our own and before which we therefore recoil in a wonder that strikes us chill and numb.

(*The Idea of the Holy*, 1917)

Otto presents the *tremendum* component of the numinous experience as comprising three elements:

- *Awefulness* – inspiring awe, a sort of profound unease.
- *Overpoweringness* – that which, among other things, inspires a feeling of humility.
- *Energy or urgency* – creating an impression of immense vigour, compelling.

The *mysterium* component has two elements:

- *Wholly other* – totally outside our normal experience.
- *Fascination* – causes the subject of the experience to be caught up in it.

In his book, Otto illustrates this type of experience by examples from mostly Christian sources. He expresses a particular view about religious development, concluding that 'Christianity ... stands out in complete superiority over all sister religions' (page 142).

The importance of the non-rational numinous alongside the rise of the rational in the Judaeo-Christian tradition is also seen as key and Otto traces these aspects in the Bible. For instance fear and terror is the experience of Moses at the Burning Bush in Exodus 3:6 'At this, Moses hid his face, because he was afraid to look at God', and the culmination of the idea of the 'holy' is seen in the Prophets and the Gospels. Likewise Isaiah's vision:

> 'Woe is me!' I cried. 'I am ruined! For I am a man of unclean lips, and I live among a people of unclean lips, and my eyes have seen the King, the Lord Almighty'.

> *(Isaiah 6:5)*

The calling of Simon Peter in Luke 5:8 again shows this deep conviction of unworthiness and the need to be cleansed:

> Go away from me, Lord; I am a sinful man!

The aspect of awe and dread and resulting humility of the numinous experience can be seen in the writings of Julian of Norwich:

> ... the whole creation, wondering and astonished, will have for God a dread so great and reverent and beyond anything known before, that the very pillars of heaven will tremble and quake ... as they marvel at the greatness of God their Maker, and the insignificance of all that is made. The consideration of all this makes the creature wonderfully meek and mild.

> *(Revelations, Chapter 75)*

This can also be found in the Hindu tradition, for example the revelation of Krishna to Arjuna in the *Bhagavad Gita* (11:25)

> Like the fire at the end of Time which burns all in the last day, I see thy vast mouths and thy terrible teeth. Where am I? Where is my shelter? Have mercy on me, God of gods, Refuge Supreme of the world.

This emphasis on the 'otherness' of God tends to put an impersonal idea at the heart of religion. In contrast Martin Buber (1878–1965) stresses personal relationships and that which underlies them. In his book (*I and Thou*, 1937) Buber argues for two kinds of relationships: the I-It and the I-Thou. The former is when we view people and things as merely phenomena. By probing more deeply we can enter the second relationship with both people and things, such that we can call it a personal relationship. 'It is here that we encounter a Thou over against our I. And this is the realm also where we encounter God'. This approach is interpreted as an experience of God through our relationships with people and the world.

## 6 Mysticism versus spirituality

It is clear that there is a growing hesitation about the use and meaning of the word 'mysticism'. McGrath (*Christian Spirituality*, 1999) argues that the term 'spirituality' has gained acceptance as the preferred way of referring to aspects of the devotional practices of a religion, and especially the interior individual experiences of believers. He particularly notes that the term 'mysticism' is being replaced by the term 'spirituality'. This is because 'mysticism' means very different things to different people. McGrath comments that the term has come to 'denote potentially irrational and anti-intellectual approaches to experience, often regarding apparent contradictions as a virtue' (page 6). He concludes that such unhelpful associations and misleading overtones make the use of the word problematic.

Similarly Bauerschmidt (*Why the Mystics Matter Now*, 2003) writes:

> My word processor's thesaurus gives the following synonyms for 'mysticism': cabalism, occult, supernatural, voodoo, witchcraft. ... I am tempted to conclude that the words have become so vague and misleading that we should simply discard them. ... but words are notoriously difficult to take out of circulation by decree.

## Answering questions on Chapter 3

By the end of this chapter you should know and understand the main features of mystical experiences, and be able to illustrate them. You should be aware of the debate as to whether the mystical experiences from different cultures are basically the same type or significantly different types. In addition, you should understand the term 'numinous' and be able to illustrate it.

Clearly not all the features that appear in the various lists occur in every mystical experience. It would be absurd to expect this. Therefore a number of quotes may be required if the features of a mystical experience are to be illustrated and discussed.

A typical AS question might be *Explain what is meant by a mystical experience*.

One of the problems of answering exam questions on mysticism is that there is a vast amount of material available. As a result, candidates have difficulties selecting appropriate material and tend to write over-long answers. This means that there is less time to answer other questions and so this will penalise the candidate.

Another common error in answering exam questions is that candidates tend to learn lists of characteristics/features (e.g. those given by James, Happold and Pahnke). It would be impossible to deal with such a long list in the time available for the AS question given above. Candidates who attempt this end up giving a list without explanation and as little understanding has been shown, only a low-level grade can be awarded. What is required is not a list but clear explanations that are then illustrated and commented on. It is also important to show the recognition of diversity within mysticism is (e.g. theistic, monistic, nature).

As with all questions on religious experience, it is key that good illustrations are selected to exemplify the discussion about characteristics, features and so on. Therefore it is worth learning a few that can be commented on and that will illustrate key points. All too often candidates learn quotes from, say, Teresa of Avila, but think that a quote without comment will suffice as an explanation.

One phenomenon sometimes associated with an intense mystic experience is the occurrence of stigmata. According to the *Encyclopedia Britannica*: 'Stigmata is a phenomenon observed in a number of Christian saints and mystics for which no satisfactory natural explanation has been offered yet. It consists of the appearance, on the body of a living person, of wounds or scars corresponding to those of the crucified Christ. The first and most celebrated stigmatization of this kind is that of St Francis of Assisi'. There are many websites that discuss this phenomenon.

Experiments carried out with human cadavers in the 1930s through to the 1950s by the French surgeon Pierre Barbet supposedly showed that the hands alone are not able support the weight of a crucified body. It has therefore been suggested that a nail penetrated the wrist (between the radius and ulna) rather than the palm or through an area called 'destot's space'. Interestingly, since the early middle ages, the crucified Christ has traditionally been depicted with nails driven through the palms of the hands. However, in more recent times, some stigmatics have exhibited wounds in their wrists instead of the palm of the hand. How would you argue that this does **not** show that stigmatas are caused by the power of the mind?

# 4 Conversion

**KEY WORDS**

**Friends of the Western Buddhist Order (FWBO)** – a Buddhist movement that was founded in the UK in 1967
**idealism** – the doctrine that ideas, or thought, are the fundamental reality
**Jesus Army** – the outreach ministry of the Jesus Fellowship Church, known for its colourful street evangelism and community lifestyle
**pantheism** – the idea that the whole universe is God or part of God
**sadhu** – a Hindu holy man
**theism** – the belief in a personal deity, creator of everything that exists and who is distinct from that creation

## 1 What is a religious conversion?

The government in the Indian state of Gujarat has decided to bring in a new law to stop the practice of religious conversion. The law – known as Dharam Swatantrata Vidheya – will be similar to anti-conversion laws that exist in some other Indian states.

> In December police arrested a number of people who were organising a mass ceremony. Thousands of low-caste Hindus – known as Dalits – were due to convert to Christianity and Buddhism.
>
> The event was organised in direct defiance of a tough new anti-conversion law, similar to the one planned by the Gujarat authorities. The recent conversion of whole low-caste Hindu communities to other religions alarmed Hindu organisations.
>
> In Tamil Nadu, Hindu leaders accused evangelical Christians of bribing the poor by offering inducements to convert and they saw the new law as a way of protecting them. During the last few years several instances of Christians being targeted for attempting to convert tribal groups have been reported from Gujarat.

Is this a true news report? Or fictional? How did you decide?

In fact it comes from the news page of the BBC website for 25 February 2003. What issues does it raise about the subject of religious conversion?

## a) William James' definition

> **KEY QUESTION** What is meant by conversion?

The word 'conversion' means 'to change direction' or 'to turn around'. McGuire (*Religion: The Social Context*, 1997) defined it as 'a process of religious change which transforms the way the individual perceives the rest of society and his or her personal place in it, altering one's view of the world'.

James devotes three chapters in his book to discussions about religious conversions, using several examples from a study made of conversions by his one-time student, Starbuck. However his understanding and analysis of the experience is from the perspective of a psychologist who interprets conversions in terms of a psychological mechanism rather than a miraculous occurrence. Hence he uses phrases such as 'the unifying of the inner self'. According to James, it is the fruits of the life that result from the conversion experience that give it positive value and he suggests that conversion could be a good thing – even if it can be explained in terms of natural psychology. For alternative understandings of the experience see Section 2 below.

James saw religious experience as a key feature of conversion. He defined the term at the start of Lecture 9 in his book *The Varieties of Religious Experience*:

> To be converted, to be regenerated, to receive grace, to experience religion, to gain an assurance, are so many phrases which denote the *process, gradual or sudden*, by which a *self hitherto divided*, and consciously wrong, inferior and unhappy, becomes unified and consciously right, superior and happy, in consequence of its firmer hold upon religious realities.

## b) Key features of his definition

Even though James understood the conversion only in psychological terms, his definition of the experience does cover some key general features of the phenomenon.

### i) A process
As a psychologist, James claims that in all of us there is 'a normal evolution of character which chiefly consists in the straightening out and unifying of the inner self ... while this organisation is taking place, there tends to be unhappiness'.

### ii) Gradual or sudden
The classic example of a sudden conversion is that of Saul (later named Paul), recorded in the New Testament:

As he neared Damascus on his journey, suddenly a light from heaven flashed around him. He fell to the ground and heard a voice say to him, 'Saul, Saul, why do you persecute me?'

'Who are you, Lord?' Saul asked.

'I am Jesus, whom you are persecuting', he replied. 'Now get up and go into the city, and you will be told what you must do'. The men travelling with Saul stood there speechless; they heard the sound but did not see anyone.

(*Acts* 9:3–7)

Paul's conversion and subsequent radical life change was based on a direct religious experience, rather than the authority of the Church or intellectual debate (Galatians 1:16–17; 1 Corinthians 1:20–25).

Even in cases of apparent sudden conversions, James suggested that there will have been prior sub-conscious development. Given that the context of Paul's conversion is that he was on his way to persecute Christians and had just previously witnessed the stoning of Stephen, can you make out a case for Paul's conversion **not** being sudden?

The Christian twentieth-century evangelist Billy Graham agreed that conversion did not have to be an instant dateable experience, but it did have to be a conscious experience, a real experience:

Whether they can remember the time or not, there was a moment when they crossed over the line from death to life. You cannot tell the exact moment when night becomes day, but you know when it is daylight.

(*World Aflame*, 1966)

### iii) Self divided becomes unified

Again, the conversion experience is understood from a psychological perspective by James. He sees this aspect illustrated by two types of the divided self, both reflecting an awareness of incompleteness:

- '*sick souls*' – those who are driven by a feeling of two lives, the natural and the spiritual, and who must lose one before they can participate in the other. He quotes from John Bunyan's autobiography as an example:

  And now I was sorry that God had made me a man. The beasts, birds, fishes etc., I blessed their condition, for they had not a sinful nature; they were not obnoxious to the wrath of God; they were not to go to hell-fire after death. I could have rejoiced, had my condition been as any of theirs.

  (*The Varieties of Religious Experience*, page 164)

- '*healthy minded*' – those who see two selves, one actual and one ideal. The battle is to strive for the ideal. James expresses it as 'Happiness and religious peace consist in living on the plus side of the account … and eliminating the minuses from life'.

## iv) Volitional or self-surrendering

In the case of self-surrender the individual must give up, relinquish, his or her personal will. Although an individual may resist, it is not until surrender that the conversion takes place. James notes that often in these instances, the state of sin is such that the individual is obsessed with escaping from it and only self-surrender will achieve it. A good example is cited by James (page 211):

> I finally ceased to resist, and gave myself up, though it was a hard struggle. Gradually the feeling came over me that I had done my part, and God was willing to do his.

Finney's experience is an example of volitional conversion and is cited by James (page 210). In some ways the volitional is similar to the self-surrendering in that there must come a point in every conversion where the personal will must be given up, but without the resistance or battle that is characteristic of the self-surrender.

## v) Passive or active

Passive conversion is where the subject has a religious experience without deliberately seeking it. The experience comes upon them unexpectedly. Again, Paul's conversion on the road to Damascus is a good example. He was passive in that it happened to him without him initiating it through meditation or some religious ritual.

Active conversion is when someone might specifically seek a spiritual experience, perhaps by going to an evangelistic meeting with the intention of responding to the preaching.

## vi) Transforming

It is through the passing from one state of being to another that a person may experience the kind of transforming process that can be described as conversion. However, Paul's conversion was not putting on a patch of holiness, but rather it was holiness woven into all his power, principles and practice. He described himself as a new man, a new creation (2 Corinthians 5:17). Donovan (*Interpreting Religious Experience*, 1979) gives an example from Islam:

> Everything seemed clear now, everything made sense to me, and I began to understand myself, the Universe and Allah ... . My whole world was shattered in one instant; all concepts had to be revised.

## c) Results of a conversion

James concludes his survey of conversion with an analysis of the symptoms felt by the converts:

- The loss of worry, the sense that all is ultimately well with one's being.
- The sense of perceiving truths not known before.

- A sense of clean and beautiful newness within and without.
- The ecstasy of happiness produced.

However there are many who have had a conversion experience for whom the symptoms are not present. How radical the change actually is in a person's life varies, and there are also cases where the person later leaves the faith.

Symbolic religious rituals often follow the conversion experience and include joining with the faith community. For Christians, rituals can include baptism or confirmation. These serve to give public testimony and cement the change. In Judaism there are two ritual requirements:

- A male convert must undergo circumcision, and if they are already circumcised, a single drop of blood is drawn as a symbolic circumcision.
- The convert must undergo immersion in a Jewish ritual bath (a mikveh), with appropriate prayers.

## 2 Types of conversion

Conversion is a broad term and covers a variety of circumstances. The following looks at three possible types:

### a) Conversion from no religion to a faith

An example of this is Augustine (354–430 CE). In his *Confessions* he wrote:

> I probed the hidden depths of my soul and wrung its pitiful secrets from it, and when I mustered them all before the eyes of my heart, a great storm broke within me, bringing with it a great deluge of tears. I stood up and left Alypius so that I might weep and cry to my heart's content, for it occurred to me that tears were best shed in solitude. ... when all at once I heard the singing of a child in a nearby house. Whether it was the voice of a boy or a girl I cannot say, but again and again it repeated the refrain 'Take it and read, take it and read'. At this I looked up, thinking hard whether there was a game in which children chant words like these, but I could not remember ever hearing them before. I stemmed my flood of tears and stood up, telling myself that this could only be a divine command to open my book of Scripture and read the first passage on which my eyes should fall. ... So I hurried back to the place where Alypius was sitting, for when I stood up to move away I had put down the book containing Paul's Epistles. I seized it and opened it, and in silence I read the first passage on which my eyes fell: *Not in revelling and drunkenness, not in lust and wantonness, not in quarrels and rivalries. Rather, arm yourselves with the Lord Jesus Christ; spend no more thought on nature and nature's appetites.* I had no wish to read more and no need

to do so. For in an instant, as I came to the end of the sentence, it was as though the light of confidence flooded into my heart and all the darkness of doubt was dispelled.

(Book VIII, 12)

Augustine, intent on breaking wholly with his old life, wrote to Ambrose to ask for baptism.

Another example is the conversion of the singer/writer Yusuf Islam (formerly Cat Stevens). He had been searching and rejected various religions. He recounts:

I tried Zen and Ching, numerology, tarot cards and astrology. I tried to look back into the Bible and could not find anything. At this time I did not know anything about Islam, and then, what I regarded as a miracle occurred. My brother had visited the mosque in Jerusalem and was greatly impressed that while on the one hand it throbbed with life (unlike the churches and synagogues which were empty), on the other hand, an atmosphere of peace and tranquillity prevailed.

When he came to London he brought back a translation of the Qur'an, which he gave to me. He did not become a Muslim, but he felt something in this religion, and thought I might find something in it also. And when I received the book, a guidance that would explain everything to me – who I was; what was the purpose of life; what was the reality and what would be the reality; and where I came from – I realized that this was the true religion ... . The first thing I wanted to do now was to be a Muslim. I realized that everything belongs to God, that slumber does not overtake Him. He created everything. ... At this point I started discovering my faith. I felt I was a Muslim.

In both of these examples the person had some beliefs but not a religion as such. Only at their conversions did they align themselves with a religion.

The conversion of CS Lewis is another one that emphasises the intellectual component of the decision rather than the emotional. His intellectual search progressed 'from "popular realism" [atheism] to Philosophical Idealism; from **Idealism** to **Pantheism**; from Pantheism to **Theism**; and from Theism to Christianity'.

On 21 December 1929, Lewis, upon reading John Bunyan's *Grace Abounding*, wrote: 'I ... am still finding more and more the element of truth in the old beliefs [that] I feel I cannot dismiss ... There must be something in it; only what?' In this pre-conversion period Lewis wrote: 'I felt as if I were a man of snow at long last beginning to melt'. As a result, in 1929 Lewis was converted to theism. He wrote of that experience: 'I gave in, and admitted that God was God, and knelt and prayed; perhaps, that night the most dejected and reluctant convert in all England', but this conversion 'was only to Theism. I knew nothing about the Incarnation'.

Lewis's autobiography speaks primarily of his conversion to theism (in 1929) rather than of his conversion to Christianity (in 1931). The critical change came in September 1931. The night of 19 September, Lewis walked and talked (until around 4 a.m.) with JRR Tolkien and Hugo Dyson about myth and Christianity. On 28 September 1931, aged 32, Lewis was:

> riding to the Whipsnade zoo in the sidecar of Warren's motorcycle. When we set out I did not believe that Jesus Christ is the Son of God, and when we reached the zoo I did. According to I John 5:1 and 5, all those who believe that Jesus is the Son of God are 'born of God'.

Lewis wrote to Arthur Greeves on 1 October 1931: 'I have just passed from believing in God to definitely believing in Christ – in Christianity'.

The emotional element of conversion is well expressed by the poem *The Hound of Heaven* by Francis Thompson. Part of this poem expresses the feeling of being pursued by God.

> I fled Him, down the nights and down the days;
> I fled Him, down the arches of the years;
> I fled Him, down the labyrinthine ways
> Of my own mind; and in the midst of tears
> I hid from Him, and under running laughter.
> Up vistaed hopes, I sped;
> And shot precipitated,
> Adown Titanic glooms of chasmèd fears,
> From those strong Feet that followed, followed after.
> But with unhurrying chase,
> And unperturbèd pace,
> Deliberate speed, majestic instancy,
> They beat – and a Voice beat,
> More instant than the Feet:
> 'All things betray thee, who betrayest Me.'

> Alack! Thou knowest not
> How little worthy of any love thou art!
> Whom wilt thou find to love ignoble thee,
> Save Me, save only Me?
> All which I took from thee, I did but take,
> Not for thy harms,
> But just that thou might'st seek it in my arms.
> All which thy child's mistake
> Fancies as lost, I have stored for thee at home:
> 'Rise, clasp My hand, and come!'

> Halts by me that footfall.
> Is my gloom, after all,
> Shade of His hand, outstretched caressingly?
> 'Ah, fondest, blindest, weakest,
> I am He whom thou seekest!
> Thou dravest Love from thee, who dravest Me.'

Francis Thompson felt that he had been running away from God but God had pursued him relentlessly until he caught up with him. He saw his conversion as the moment when 'the Hound of Heaven' had overtaken him and he had surrendered himself to God. He became a practising Catholic.

## b) Conversion from one faith to another

An example is Sundar Singh (1889–1929), who was raised a devout Sikh, and consecrated from his youth to become a Hindu **sadhu**. A sadhu is a Hindu who devotes his entire life to his religion and forsakes all the worldly pleasures. Sundar claimed that his conversion contained the following sequences, which are very similar to those of Paul (see earlier).

Emotional and spiritual turmoil drove Sundar to ask God to reveal Himself fully, lest he take his own life in the hope of finding peace in his future reincarnation. When he did so he looked up and was surprised to see a faint cloud of light in the room. It was too early for the dawn. He opened the door and peered out to the courtyard. Darkness. Turning back into the room he saw that the light in the room was getting brighter. At first he feared that the room was on fire. But nothing happened. While watching the light, he suddenly saw Jesus' figure – not the face of any of his traditional gods, but of Jesus. Jesus was there in the room, shining, radiating an inexpressible joy and peace and love, looking at him with compassion and asking, 'Why do you persecute me? I died for you ...' [Acts 9:1–5]. At that time, Sundar realised that Jesus was not dead but alive. Sundar fell on his knees before Him and experienced an astonishing peacefulness that he had never felt before. Sundar was later baptised.

## c) Conversion from faith (believing) to faith (trusting)

A good example is the conversion of the reformer Martin Luther (1483–1546), who was a monk and a priest.

After meditating day and night, finally the breakthrough came when Luther gave heed to the words at the end of Romans 1:17, 'He who through faith is righteous shall live'. Then he came to believe that the verse was not talking about the active deeds of righteousness that God demands, but the righteousness that comes from being absolved from sin through Christ's atoning death. The sinner is justified (declared righteous) by God through faith in the work and death of Jesus, not by keeping the Law. Put another way, the sinner is justified by faith (receiving) rather than works (achieving).

This, according to Luther, was a conversion experience. When he had discovered that God gives His righteousness as a gift in Christ, he felt that he 'was altogether born again and had entered paradise itself through open gates ... that place in Paul was for me truly the gate to

John Wesley preaching

paradise'. Now his conscience was at rest, now he was certain of his salvation.

Another similar conversion is that of John Wesley (1703–91), the clergyman who founded the Methodist Movement. He was aware that he did not have a faith in Christ as a personal saviour that he saw others had. However on 24 May 1738, at a meeting of an evangelical society in Aldersgate, London, he had a conversion experience. He wrote in his journal for that day:

> In the evening I went very unwillingly to a society, where one was reading Luther's preface to the Epistle to the Romans. About a quarter before nine, while he was describing the change which God works in the heart through faith in Christ, I felt my heart strangely warmed. I felt I did trust in Christ, Christ alone, for salvation: and an assurance was given me, that he had taken away my sins, even mine, and saved me from the law of sin and death.

Both Luther and Wesley saw their conversions as a movement from academic acceptance to personal trust.

## 3 Conversion motifs

As has already been highlighted, religious conversions are very varied. In 1981 John Lofland and Norman Skonovd (*Journal for the Scientific*

*Study of Religion*, 20, 1981) described six patterns (motifs) of religious conversion. The list has been summarised by Moojan Momen (*The Phenomenon of Religion*, 1999):

- *Intellectual* – emphasis is on intensive study with little interpersonal contact.
- *Mystical* – occurs suddenly and dramatically, accompanied sometimes by dreams or visions.
- *Experimental* – emphasis is on active exploration, assessing the religion over a period of time through participation.
- *Affectional* – involves contact and bonding with actual members of the religion and experiencing being loved and nurtured.
- *Revivalist* – occurs in a revivalist meeting. Usually involves emotional arousal.
- *Coercive* – persuasion and thought programming. New religious movements are sometimes accused of this, though it is doubtful whether they are guilty. Another form of this involves financial or social status enticements.

Consider which motif each of the following accounts of conversion illustrates.

> ... I found the opportunity I had long wished for, of attending a camp meeting ... One of the preachers ... assured us of the enormous depravity of man ... and of his perfect sanctification after he had wrestled sufficiently with the Lord to get hold of him. The preachers came down from their stand ... and, beginning to sing a hymn, called penitents to come forth ...
>
> *(Religious Experience: A Sociological Perspective, 1996)*
>
> Emily recollected how she was impressed by the Muslim family that she knew ... At that time I was seeing the Muslim family and I was watching and listening to what they said and what they did. I was trying to see how they were different. They were very sincere in their faith and they were friendly in this materialistic and selfish society. That really helped towards my reversion.
>
> *(Conversion to Islam, 1996)*
>
> I retired to rest soon after I got home, and felt indifferent to the things of religion until I began to be exercised by the Holy Spirit, which began in about five minutes after, in the following manner:
> At first I began to feel my heart beat very quick all on a sudden, which made me at first think that perhaps something is going to ail me, though I was not alarmed, for I felt no pain ... I began to feel exceedingly happy and humble, and such a sense of unworthiness as I never felt before ... My heart seemed as if it would burst, but it did not stop until I felt as if I was unutterably full of the love and

grace of God. In the meantime, while thus exercised, a thought arose in my mind, what can it mean? And all at once, as if to answer it, my memory became exceedingly clear, and it appeared to me just as if the New Testament was placed open before me, eighth chapter of Romans, and as light as if some candle lighted was held for me to read the 26th and 27th verses of the chapter ... I lay reflecting ... feeling as if my soul was full of the Holy Spirit ... When I awoke in the morning ... my soul felt as completely raised above the fears of death as of going to sleep; and like a bird in a cage, I had a desire, if it was the will of God, to get released from my body and to dwell with Christ, though willing to live to do good to others, and to warn sinners to repent ... I went downstairs ... to the shelf and looked into the testament, at the eighth of Romans, and every verse seemed to almost speak and to confirm it to be truly the Word of God, and as if my feelings corresponded with the meaning of the words ... After breakfast I went round to converse with my neighbours on religion, which I could not have been hired to have done before this, and at their request I prayed with them, though I had never prayed in public before.

*(The Varieties of Religious Experience)*

Brad from Texas and of a Southern Baptist upbringing, began to question his base in Christianity at approximately age 12. Over the years he abandoned all aspects of organized religion then, feeling a spiritual void, he began to study the various religions of the world. Through this study he came to develop his own philosophy, his definition of God, and began to establish what his relationship with God was to be. He found that the product of his search was what Judaism is. Brad describes his process to conversion as, 'wandering in the desert for many years before determining that (his) beliefs coincided with those of Judaism'. He undertook formal conversion at age 51.

*(http://www.convertingtojudaism.com/Personal-Conversion-Experiences.htm)*

# 4 Stages of conversion

Lofland and Stark (*American Social Review*, 30, 1965) gave a conversion process model of seven stages. Like the conversion motifs above, there is overlap, however they do provide a good summary of the key features. Keishin Inaba from Kobe University, Japan, applied this conversion process model using studies on two new religious movements: the **Jesus Army** and **Friends of the Western Buddhist Order (FWBO)** (*Human Sciences Research*, 11, 2004). The seven stages identified are:

- *Tension* – the Jesus Army evangelises homeless people on the streets and Inaba found that over 50% in his survey of Jesus Army interviewees had been experiencing tensions when they met the Jesus Army.
- *Religious problem-solving perspective* – potential converts seek solutions within a religious perspective. Many converts of the FWBO were initially interested in meditation and then gradually progressed to Buddhism.
- *Seekership* – potential converts become religious seekers. For instance an FWBO convert said 'My stepmother had died about a year earlier, so I had also had an experience of grief, which I think was also a factor making me want to explore what life was about'. Likewise a Jesus Army convert commented 'my wife and I were looking for something deeper … we were longing for greater spiritual depth'.
- *Turning point* – pre-converts perceived a turning point in their lives shortly before or concurrently with their encounter with the new religious movement. These situations saw new involvements as possible and desirable. Interestingly, Inaba did not find this feature reflected in the people he interviewed from the Jesus Army and the FWBO.
- *Affective bond* – the formation of a strong bond between the believer and the potential convert is an important factor in the conversion process. This close personal relationship helps the potential convert to feel accepted and overcome any conflicts. A Jesus Army convert said 'What really attracted me was the sincerity of the people, and the obvious love and bonding that they had with each other. I wanted to be part of it and the life that I could get from it'. Inaba reported that overall, affective bonds facilitated conversions of over 96% of the Jesus Army interviewees and over 76% of the FWBO interviewees.
- *Weak extra-cult attachments* – the Unification Church (Moonies) were known for moving potential converts away from their homes and surrounding them with a new environment.
- *Intensive interaction* – new friendships and bonds are developed amongst the believers so that a new 'family' is formed. A Jesus Army convert commented on 'the spiritual power that I felt here, also the sense of family, the brotherhood'.

## 5 Psychological or divine or both?

Clearly there are many and varied opinions as to the extent to which religious conversion is a psychological or spiritual phenomenon. The reader will judge the matter in light of their own religious beliefs or lack of them. In the accounts listed in this chapter it does seem that some conversions are through an intellectual choice while others are more emotional. This may suggest that psychological explanations may not be the full account of the religious event. For further discussion on these issues see Chapters 9 and 10.

## Answering questions on Chapter 4

By the end of this chapter you should know and be able to illustrate/comment on the key features of a conversion experience. In addition you should understand the different types of conversion and be able to give examples. Although this chapter does not discuss whether a religious conversion is a psychological or a spiritual phenomenon, it should be noted that this evaluative aspect often forms part of the exam question. Indeed the opening section of the chapter should have raised questions as to whether people can be made to convert and whether you can stop people converting. These issues are discussed in Chapters 9 and 10.

A typical exam question would be *Explain what is meant by a conversion experience*.

The need in the exam to have good examples of conversions that illustrate the key features cannot be stressed enough. Once again, just recounting a conversion without explanation and comment will only achieve lower level marks. Equally just listing key features will be insufficient to gain a pass grade at AS/A2.

On page 31 the question was raised as to whether Paul's conversion illustrated a sudden experience. The features are not always clear. For instance some commentators argue that Paul had already been a Christian for a long time, but was unconscious of the fact. His fanaticism is claimed as evidence that he had had doubts about his persecution of Christians. Some would claim Paul's conversion was more psychological than spiritual.

The common motifs that are illustrated on pages 38–39 are (i) revivalist, (ii) affectional, (iii) mystical and (iv) intellectual.

Although not discussed in the chapter, the Buddha's 'four sights' can be used as an example of a conversion experience. The account of this event claims that as Siddhattha grew more discontented he asked his charioteer to take him on an excursion outside the palace. On the first visit he encountered an old man. On the next excursion he encountered a sick man. On his third excursion, he encountered a corpse being carried to cremation. Such sights brought home to him the prevalence of suffering in the world and that he too was subject to old age, sickness and death – that no-one, not even a king's son, could escape these three. What hope was there, what point in living, if this was the destiny of all? On his fourth excursion, however, he encountered a holy man or sadhu, apparently content and at peace with the world. He then began to think that perhaps there was an answer to what seemed like the inevitability of suffering and so he set out on his quest that eventually led to his enlightenment (Buddha means 'the enlightened one').

Another interesting account of a conversion experience is the poem *The Everlasting Mercy* by John Masefield. It tells of the conversion of Saul Kane and the changes that come into his life. You might also consider reading Acts

8:26–40. This is the account of the conversion of the Ethiopian official. What key features of conversion are illustrated and what conversion motif does it exemplify?

The material in this chapter is useful when considering the role and importance of religious experience. For sections on faith and moral behaviour see Chapter 11.

# 5 Visions

A vision can be defined as something seen other than by ordinary sight, i.e. supernatural or prophetic sight experienced usually in sleep or ecstasy – especially one that conveys a revelation. Hence it sometimes overlaps with mystical experiences (Chapter 3), conversion (Chapter 4), revelation (Chapter 6) and near-death experience (Chapter 7).

**KEY QUESTION** What are the main features of visions?

## 1 What are visions about?

### a) An image or event in which there is a message

In Acts 10:9–16 Peter had a vision of heaven opening and a large sheet, containing all kinds of four-footed animals, as well as reptiles and birds, being let down to earth. He then heard a voice saying, 'Get up Peter. Kill and eat'. When Peter protested because the items were unclean the voice said 'Do not call anything impure that God has made clean'.

Find out what Peter understood to be the meaning of this vision by reading Acts, Chapter 11.

### b) Religious figures

Joan of Arc said that one of her visions was of Saint Michael.

> It was Saint Michael, who I saw before my eyes; he was not alone, but was accompanied by many angels from Heaven … I saw them with my bodily eyes, as well as I am seeing you; and when they left, I wept and greatly wished that they should have taken me with them.
>
> Saint Michael, when he came to me, told me that Saint Catherine and Saint Margaret would come to me and that I should act on their advice; that they were instructed to lead and advise me in what I had to do; and that I should believe in what they would say to me, for it was by God's order.

Whereas Joan of Arc had a vision of a saint, Teresa of Avila had a vision of Jesus himself.

When Teresa of Avila was 40 she claimed to experience a series of visions, 'seen not with the eyes of the body but the eyes of the soul'. She recounted that:

> One day, when I was at prayer, the Lord was pleased to reveal to me nothing but His hands, the beauty of which was so great as to be indescribable ... A few days later I also saw that Divine face, which seemed to leave me completely absorbed.

And finally:

> There stood before me the most sacred Humanity in the full beauty and majesty of His resurrected body ...

The visions were lit by an unearthly light:

> It is a light so different from what we know here below that the sun's brightness seems dim by comparison ... It is like looking upon very clear water running over a bed of crystal and reflecting the sun, compared with a very muddy stream running over the earth beneath a cloudy sky. It seems rather to be natural light, whereas the other is artificial.

Teresa of Avila's most famous vision became the subject of the statue by Bernini:

> I would see beside me, on my left hand, an angel in bodily form ... He was not tall, but short, and very beautiful, his face so aflame that he appeared to be one of the highest types of angel who seem to be all afire ... In his hands I saw a long golden spear and at the end of the iron tip I seemed to see a point of fire. With this he seemed to pierce my heart several times so that it penetrated to my entrails. When he drew it out, I thought he was drawing them out with it and he left me completely afire with a great love for God. The pain was so sharp that it made me utter several moans; and so excessive was the sweetness caused me by the intense pain that one can never wish to lose it, nor will one's soul be content with anything less than God.

## c) Places (heaven and hell)

Sikhism contains an example of a vision of God's court. It is said that one morning Nanak failed to return from his ablutions. His clothes were found on the river bank and the townspeople concluded that he had drowned. Daulat Khan had the river dragged but no body was discovered. After three days Nanak reappeared but remained silent. It was the next day before he spoke and then he made the pronouncement:

> There is neither Hindu nor Muslim so whose path shall I follow? I shall follow God's path. God is neither Hindu nor Muslim and the path which I follow is God's

*(Majh ki Var Mohalla* 1, page 141)

Explaining what had happened to him he said that he was taken to the court of God and escorted into his presence. There a cup was filled with armrit (nectar) and was given to him with the command, 'This is the cup of the adoration of God's name. Drink it. I am with you. I bless you and raise you up. Whoever remembers you will enjoy my favour. Go, rejoice in my name and teach others to do so. I have bestowed the gift of my name upon you. Let this be your calling'.

A passage in the Guru Granth Sahib is said to be another description of his experience.

I was a minstrel out of work,
The Lord gave me employment.
The mighty One instructed me,
'Night and day, sing my praise.'
The Lord summoned the minstrel
To his High Court.
On me he bestowed the robe of honouring him and singing his praise.
On me he bestowed the Nectar in a cup,
The nectar of his true and holy name.
Those who at the bidding of the Guru Feast
And take their fill of the Lord's holiness
Attain peace and joy.
Your minstrel spreads your glory
By singing your word. Nanak, through adoring the truth
We attain to the all-highest.

(Adi Granth 150)

There is also evidence of favourable and unfavourable aspects to an 'afterlife' in many of the reported apparitions of Mary. One of the most well known of these occurred at Fatima, Portugal, in 1917. The visionaries reported a vision of hell. As Lucia, one of the visionaries, described it:

... we saw as it were a sea of fire. Plunged in this fire were demons and souls in human form, like transparent burning embers, all blackened or burnished bronze, floating about in the conflagration, now raised into the air by the flames that issued from within themselves together with great clouds of smoke, now falling back on every side like sparks in huge fires, without weight or equilibrium, amid shrieks and groans of pain and despair, which horrified us and made us tremble with fear. The demons could be distinguished by their terrifying and repellent likeness to frightful and unknown animals, black and transparent like burning coals.

## d) Fantastic creatures/figures

The prophet Ezekiel recounts a vision he had:

... and in the fire was what looked like four living creatures. In appearance their form was that of a man, but each of them had four faces and four wings ... Each of the four had the face of a man, and on the right side each had the face of a lion, and on the left the face of an ox; each also had the face of an eagle ...

(*Ezekiel* 1:6, 10)

### e) Future (end of world/final judgement)

The Book of Revelation contains John's visions of the final judgement.

Another book was opened, which is the book of life. The dead were judged according to what they had done as recorded in the books. The sea gave up the dead that were in it, and death and Hades gave up the dead that were in them, and each person was judged according to what he had done. Then death and Hades were thrown into the lake of fire. The lake of fire is the second death. If anyone's name was not found written in the book of life, he was thrown into the lake of fire.

(*Revelations* 20:12–15)

## 2  Types of visions

It is usual to divide visions into different types. Labelling them in this way is not meant to be a comment on their validity or otherwise.

### a) Group visions

These are visions that are seen by more than one person.

During the First World War it was reported that a miracle had happened during the British Army's clash with the advancing Germans at Mons in Belgium. In some versions a vision of St George and a phantom bowman halted the Kaiser's troops, while others claimed angels had thrown a protective curtain around the British, saving them from disaster. The battle of Mons took place on 23 August 1914 and within weeks news of the 'angels of Mons' had spread far and wide.

### b) Individual visions

These are visions that are seen by only one person. This happens in the vast majority of cases. An interesting case is that claimed by Bernadette of Lourdes.

On Thursday, 11 February 1858, Bernadette Soubirous was searching for wood when she heard a loud noise like the sound of a storm coming from a nearby grotto. At the entrance of the grotto was a rosebush which was moving as if it were windy, which it was not. From the interior of the grotto she saw a golden-coloured cloud, and soon after a lady, young and beautiful was at the entrance of the opening above the rosebush. The lady smiled at Bernadette and motioned for her to

Angels of Mons

advance. Bernadette lost any fear she may have had and fell to her knees to pray before the **rosary**. After both she and the lady had completed these prayers, the lady slowly withdrew to the interior of the grotto and disappeared.

Bernadette claimed to have experienced 18 visitations from Mary over a six-month period, not knowing who the lady was until the last apparition. During the apparitions, Mary instructed Bernadette to dig a hole in the ground and drink and bathe in it. The hole later turned into a spring of water, which Mary promised would be a healing spring for all who came to use its waters. Mary also asked Bernadette to tell the local priest to have a chapel built in honour of her appearances there.

## c) Corporeal visions

A corporeal vision is one in which the object is external but only visible to certain people. These are usually visions of angels that are not appearances just in the mind. Some people make a distinction between this and an apparition, arguing that the apparition generally appears and disappears suddenly and does not leave physical traces.

## d) Imaginative visions

This is where the image is produced in the person's imagination and has no existence external to the person. An example of this would be the visions of the final judgement recounted by John in the Book of Revelation. If they are genuine then they have been brought about by a supernatural agent. These visions are like 'pictures' sent by a divine being and often requiring some interpretation. According to the author of *The Cloud of Unknowing*, visions are generally sent to demonstrate religious truths to those who have difficulty grasping them in any other way. The author cites Stephen's vision at his martyrdom (Acts 7) where Stephen sees Christ standing in heaven and interprets this as Christ saying to Stephen 'I am standing by you spiritually' (Chapter 58).

However, discerning between corporeal and imaginative visions is problematic. Consider the following case recounted by JB Phillips:

> The late C.S. Lewis, whom I did not know very well, and had only seen in the flesh once, but with whom I had corresponded a fair amount, gave me an unusual experience. A few days after his death, while I was watching television, he 'appeared' sitting in a chair within a few feet of me, and spoke a few words which were particularly relevant to the difficult circumstances through which I was passing. He was ruddier in complexion than ever, grinning all over his face and, as the old fashioned saying has it, positively glowing with health. The interesting thing to me was that I had not been thinking about him at all. I was neither alarmed nor surprised nor... did I look up to see the hole in the ceiling that he might have made on arrival. He was just *there* – 'large as life and twice as natural!' A week later, this time when I was in bed reading before going to sleep, he appeared again, even more rosily radiant than before, and repeated to me the same message, which was very important to me at the time. I was a little puzzled by this, and I mentioned it to a certain saintly Bishop who was then living in retirement here in Dorset. His reply was, 'My dear J ... , this sort of thing is happening all the time'.
>
> (*Ring of Truth*, 1967, pages 89–90)

This is an example that highlights the difficulty in deciding the type of vision. It is not clear whether the 'appearance' of CS Lewis is just in JB Phillips' imagination. If it wasn't, then we have to decide whether the 'appearance' had an external reality or whether it had an internal 'appearance' but externally caused. If it was an external reality, was it a tangible reality (i.e. could it be touched)?

## 3 What are we to make of them?

---

**KEY QUESTION** Do any visions have an external reality?

---

As we saw in Section 2 above in the account by JB Phillips, it is difficult to assess the claimed vision. The difficulty is in assessing objectively the claims that are subjectively told. Hence people disagree. Also each claim has to be considered individually, and the evidence will weigh differently for different people, depending on their presuppositions and beliefs. As an illustration, consider two claims of visions that have been referred to in this chapter.

## a) Two case studies

### i) The angel of Mons

Some respected historians, such as AJP Taylor, give credence to the account and certainly contemporary diaries and letters show that by 1915 it had been accepted by many that a supernatural event at Mons had taken place. However the claimed 'eyewitnesses' only came forward at a later date. Others point out that if some dramatic event had occurred and the men of a particular battalion or company had seen something unusual around Mons, it would be mentioned somewhere. In the histories of the regiments most involved in the fighting there is no mention of any events that could be construed as a distraction or an intervention in the fighting. The Units that suffered most heavily on the 23rd, the 4th Royal Fusiliers and the 4th Middlesex, did not record any peculiar events whatsoever.

One theory is that the account derived from a short story by Arthur Machen called *The Bowman*. This story was a fictional description of a phantom English army led by St George marching from Agincourt in the dark days of 1914 to relieve their modern counterparts on an unidentified battlefield. *The Bowman* was published in September 1914 in the *London Evening News*. Many argue that the Bowman became 'the angel of Mons'.

### ii) Lourdes

The apparitions were declared authentic in 1862 and Lourdes rapidly became one of the world's major pilgrimage sites. It is claimed that many have been cured from a variety of illnesses, both physical and spiritual. One of the local priests accused Bernadette of lying about the apparitions and told her to find out from the lady just who she was and demanded from her that she perform a miracle by making the rosebush in the grotto bloom. On 25 March, the Feast of the Annunciation, it is claimed that Mary met the priest's request when she told Bernadette, 'I am the Immaculate Conception'. Mary, with these words, confirmed what the Pope had declared as official Catholic Church doctrine just four years earlier – this was seen as proof for many, as how could such an uneducated 14 year old in rural France know such things?

Clearly opinion on the validity of such visions is divided. Many would claim that such apparitions of Mary are superstitious throwbacks to a less enlightened time and much that was previously inexplicable can now be explained by science. Furthermore, there is a high probability that any such event is likely to be the result of wishful thinking or worse. Interestingly, there were more than 150 alleged apparitions of Mary in Europe alone in the five years following Mary's appearance at Lourdes. However, none of these was ever authenticated after subsequent investigation and analysis.

The Catholic Church, to protect itself and its members, evaluates private revelations very carefully. The process by which the Catholic Church assesses such claimed visions involves four distinct phases:

• After a thorough evaluation by a commission created by the local diocese, the bishop issues a statement of support for the event by stating that it contains nothing contrary to faith or morals, that it appears to be supernaturally inspired and that it is worthy of devotion by the faithful.
• Once approved by the bishop, a lengthy period of devotion by the faithful that results in a deepening of their faith and a return to a life of self-denial and prayer is permitted to develop. If this devotion develops and spreads, then the next stage becomes possible.
• Papal acknowledgement. The Pope states publicly that he is favourably disposed to the events and contents of the apparition.
• **Liturgical** recognition by placing celebration of the apparition on the Church's official liturgical calendar.

## b) Other explanations

Various explanations have been proposed to account for religious experiences, and these are discussed fully in Chapters 9 and 10. However visions have given rise to a particular suggestion by John of the Cross. In *Dark Night of the Soul* (2.2,3) he comments:

> ... the devil causes many to believe in vain visions and false prophecies; and strives to make them presume that God and the saints are speaking with them; and they often trust their own fancy. And the devil is also accustomed, in this state, to fill them with presumption and pride, so that they become attracted by vanity and arrogance, and allow themselves to be seen engaging in outward acts which appear holy, such as raptures and other manifestations. Thus they become bold with God, and lose holy fear, which is the key and the custodian of all the virtues; and in some of these souls so many are the falsehoods and deceits which tend to multiply, and so inveterate do they grow, that it is very doubtful if such souls will return to the pure road of virtue and true spirituality.

Likewise, Teresa of Avila makes these comments about those with a tendency to believe that they have received revelations:

Not three or four only, but a large number of people have spoken to me on the subject, and therefore I know by experience that there are souls which, either because they possess vivid imaginations or active minds, are so wrapped up in their own ideas as to feel certain that they see whatever their fancy imagines. If they had ever beheld a genuine vision, they would recognise the deception at once. They themselves fabricate, piece by piece, what they fancy they see: – no after effects are produced on the mind, which is left less moved to devotion than by the sight of a sacred picture (*Interior Castle, Sixth Mansion*, ch. ix, 6).

## Answering questions on Chapter 5

By the end of this chapter you should know some examples of the content of typical visions, and the different types such as group and imaginative. You should also be able to critically assess the claimed visions. Note that material relevant to this critical evaluation is also in Chapters 9 and 10.

A typical exam question would be *Explain what is meant by visions*.

To answer this question candidates would be expected to consider contrasting visions and to reflect some diversity. Examples to illustrate would also be expected. Questions may further ask candidates to critically evaluate claimed visions.

One of the important things to remember when critically assessing is to develop a sustained argument that moves away from just giving a list of criticisms. Two or three criticisms discussed in depth, including some response to those criticisms, is far better than just listing ten criticisms. It is also important to explain how those criticisms reveal a weakness in the argument. Many candidates tend to leave the examiner to work out why the points listed are in fact criticisms.

One useful approach when practising evaluation skills is to state what you regard as the strongest argument *against* your own personal view on the issue and then examine how you would reply to it. This develops the ability to appreciate the opposing views of an argument.

It is also important to remember that the exam is a religious studies exam, and therefore the material and examples used should have a religious context or have a religious significance. Although visions has been discussed in this chapter as a particular type of religious experience, visions can also be aspects of other types of religious experience such as mysticism or revelations. Indeed, candidates often do not treat visions as a separate category and are then in difficulty when a question is centred on this specific type. The material in this chapter is useful when discussing the role and importance of religious experiences; in particular the section on faith and practice as well as religious founders in Chapter 11, page 111.

Another possible example to use would be the Transfiguration of Jesus (Mark 9:2–10).

# 6 Revelation

---

## KEY WORDS

**mantra** – a sacred syllable or series of syllables which are recited as a form of meditation

**non-propositional revelation** – the revelation is a moment of 'realisation' coming at the end of a period of reflection and attempts to understand the significance of revelatory events

**propositional revelation** – the communication of some truth by God to humans through supernatural means which is expressed in statements or propositions

**Protestant Reformation** – a religious revolution that took place in Western Europe in the sixteenth century and ended with the establishment of Protestant Churches

---

**13 May 1917**: Lucia and two other children at Fatima claim that an apparition of Mary had appeared to them and three 'Secrets' were said to have been given to the children by Mary.

Fatima appearance

**13 May 1981**: Pope John Paul II was seriously wounded by an assassin's bullets. The Pope was saved from death when he turned to look at a young girl in the crowd wearing a picture of the Virgin of Fatima. As the Pope turned, a shot aimed at his head, missed. The Pope spoke with Lucia from his hospital room. While he was recuperating from his wounds he read everything he could about Fatima, corresponded with Lucia, and re-read the famous unreleased 'third secret'.

To find out about this third secret of Fatima and its supposed connection to the attempted assassination, check the Answering Questions section at the end of this chapter.

Certainly the events at Fatima seemed to involve some claim to a revelation. As you have seen in the preceding chapters, many forms of religious experience could be seen to involve revelation. The revelation may involve being told something very specific through supernatural means, like the claim made about Fatima, or it may involve a process through which a person gains some insight, interpreting the event.

# 1 What is revelation?

Revelation is divine self-disclosure. Through revelation, the divine becomes known to humanity. Like visions, revelation can be an aspect of any of the types of religious experience, e.g. conversion. One approach to understanding what is meant by 'revelation' is to view revelation as either **propositional** or **non-propositional**.

> **KEY QUESTION**  What is the difference between propositional and non-propositional revelation?

## a) Propositional revelation

Propositional revelation is the communication of some truth by God to humans through supernatural means. The content of this revelation is a body of truths expressed in statements or propositions. Judaism, Christianity and Islam all claim instances of such revelation. For instance, Judaism has the revelation of the Law to Moses on Mount Sinai (Exodus 19–23). In Christianity, the Bible is regarded as 'the Word of God' and in Islam, the prophet Muhammad received the Qur'an.

The account of the Qur'an being given to Muhammad is a good example of propositional revelation. Muhammad is a passive channel through whom Allah communicates.

Muhammad was 40 years old when he received his first revelation from God (610 CE) through the Angel Gabriel. This revelation, which continued for 23 years, is known as the Qur'an, the recording of the entire revelation of God. On this first appearance, Gabriel said to Muhammad: 'Iqraa', meaning read or recite. Muhammad replied, 'I cannot read', as he had not received any formal education and did not know how to read or write. The Angel Gabriel then embraced him until he reached the limit of his endurance and after releasing said: 'Iqraa'. Muhammad's answer was the same as before. Gabriel repeated the embrace for the third time, asked him to repeat after him and said:

> Recite: In the name of your Lord Who created man from a clot (of blood). Recite: Your Lord is Most Noble, Who taught by the pen, taught man what he did not know.

> (96:1–5)

This is the first verse of Surah (Chapter) 96 of the Qur'an. The revelations that he received were sometimes a few verses, a part of a chapter or the whole chapter. Some revelations came down in response to an enquiry by the non-believers. The revealed verses were recorded on a variety of available materials (leather, palm leaves, bark, shoulder bones of animals), memorised as soon as they were revealed, and were recited in daily prayers by Muslims (Qur'an 80:13–16). The Angel Gabriel taught the order and arrangement of verses, and the Prophet instructed his several scribes to record verses in that order (Qur'an 75:16–19 and 41:41–42). All the revealed verses were received over a period of 23 years until his death in 632 CE, and were compiled in the book known as the Qur'an.

Likewise in Sikhism, Guru Nanak received a revelation, which is at the start of every chapter and sub-chapter in the Sri Guru Granth Sahib (the sacred Scripture of the Sikhs). When Guru Nanak received this revelation he was still very young. He took a dip in the river alongside his house for his regular morning ablutions, but this time he disappeared into the waters, missing for two days and nights. On the third day he re-appeared from out of the water with the following verse on his lips, which is now called the Mool **Mantra** (the primordal Mantra). It is one of the most comprehensive definitions of God.

> The True One and only Omnipresent Immortal Essence of Reality. The Creator, the Omniscient and Omnipotent, the Incomprehensible (the fearless). Before all Beginnings and after all Endings. Beyond Time, Space and Form (and enmity). Free from the cycle of Births and Deaths, the Self-manifested. The Loving Merciful Enlightener (Realised with His Grace through total Submission to His Will).

## b) Non-propositional revelation

In the case of non-propositional revelation, the revelation is not a matter of Divinity imparting knowledge directly to humanity but of a moment of 'realisation' coming at the end of a period of reflection. In contrast to the propositional view that produces a body of truths about God, the non-propositional concept of revelation represents human attempts to understand the significance of revelatory events. It involves seeing or interpreting events in a special way. For instance the prophets of the Old Testament saw events in a special way, as having spiritual significance rather than just political or sociological importance. To them the Fall of Samaria or Jerusalem was an expression of judgement on Israel and its people because of disobedience. They saw God as actively at work in the world around them.

Buddhism contrasts with the theistic religions, in that the various Buddhist scriptures are not seen as emerging from some transcendent source but rather from within the Buddha himself. After six years of hardship and continual striving, the Buddha finally gained enlightenment. The profundity of this experience left him in no doubt that he had achieved final knowledge, that there was something beyond the cycle of old age, sickness and death, that there *was* an end to suffering. As he sat meditating under the Bodhi tree, he realised that he had been reborn many times; that all beings were reborn according to their deeds; that suffering was fuelled by craving and that there was a means of bringing this suffering to an end. What comes through in the scriptures is the Buddha's absolute certainty that he had attained ultimate realisation and that he knew the precise means by which others could attain it too.

# 2 Main features of revelation

According to Franks Davis (*The Evidential Force of Religious Experience*, 1989), there are five distinctive features of revelation experience:

- They are sudden and of short duration.
- Alleged new knowledge acquired immediately.
- Alleged new knowledge from external agent.
- The alleged new knowledge is received with utter conviction.
- The insights are often impossible to put into words (ineffability).

The conversion of Umar to Islam is an illustration of a revelation as he read the Qur'an. Most of the main features of revelation can be found in this account.

> The Quraish leaders called a meeting and asked for a volunteer to assassinate Muhammad [peace and blessings be upon him]. Umar offered and everybody in the meeting exclaimed that he was the right person for it. While he was on his way with a sword in his hand he met Sa'd bin Abi Waqqas who enquired of him about his destination. Umar told him that he was going to murder Muhammad [peace and blessings be upon him]. After some discussion Sa'd said, 'You had better take care of your own family first. Your sister and brother-in-law both have

accepted Islam'. Hearing this Umar changed his direction and went straight to his sister's house. When Umar knocked at the door, they were studying the Qur'an from Hadrat Khabbab (RA). His sister Fatimah was frightened on hearing Umar's voice and tried to hide the portion of the Qur'an she was reciting. When Umar entered the house he enquired about their Islam and on finding that they had accepted Islam, he first attacked his brother-in-law then, when his sister intervened he attacked her so violently on her face that it bled profusely. On this his sister burst out: 'Do whatever you like, we are determined to die as Muslims'. When Umar saw his sister bleeding, he felt ashamed. He loved Fatimah very much but could not tolerate her conversion to Islam. Umar asked her to show the pages on which the Qur'an was written. But she told him, 'You can not touch it unless you take a bath and make yourself clean'. He washed his body and then read the leaves. That was the beginning of Surah Ta Ha [Chapter 20 of the Qur'an]. When he came to the verse:

'Lo! I even I, am Allah, there is no god save Me. So serve Me and establish Salat for My remembrance'. [20:14]

Umar exclaimed, 'Surely this is the Word of Allah. Take me to Muhammad [peace and blessings be upon him]'.

On hearing this Hadrat Khabbab (RA), who had hidden himself in the house, came out from inside and said, 'O Umar! Glad tidings for you. It seems that the prayer of the Holy Prophet which he said last night has been answered in your favour'. He had prayed to Allah: 'O Allah, strengthen Islam with either Umar b. Khattab or Umar b. Hisham whomsoever Thou pleaseth'.

Umar then went to Muhammad [peace and blessings be upon him]. On seeing him, Muhammad [peace and blessings be upon him] asked him, 'Umar! what brings you here?' He said, 'I am here to accept Islam'.

*(adapted from an Al-Islaah publication about Umar with kind permission)*

As you will see, the account does not contain all the main features. There is no evidence of ineffability in connection with this particular revelation experience. Also though the experience may be sudden and short, the after-effects may last a lifetime.

## 3 The content of revelation

**KEY QUESTION** What exactly is it that is 'known'?

One of the main features listed above was acquiring new knowledge. There is a great sense of certainty and the knowing is in quite a different way from intellectual knowledge.

This seems to vary.

## a) Universal truths

In the section above, the enlightenment of Buddha was discussed. This is a good example of what he considered to be a revelation of a universal truth. It was his moment of realisation. Similarly, Guru Nanak received a universal truth revelation about the name of God.

## b) The future

Hildegard of Bingen (1098–1179) lived in a convent in Germany from the age of eight. From an early age she claimed to experience God overshadowing her life. It was not until she was 40 that she began to write down an account of the visions she had experienced. She claimed to receive insight from God about future events. An example is:

> The time is coming when princes and peoples will reject the authority of the Pope. Some countries will prefer their own Church rulers to the Pope. The German Empire will be divided.

This was claimed to be fulfilled in the sixteenth century by the **Protestant Reformation**, which resulted in the establishment of the Protestant Churches.

## c) The present

Benny Hinn, a well-known leader in the Charismatic Movement, claims that he has words of knowledge from God. For example, in front of a crowd of 18,000 people in Houston, Texas, on 9 April 1993, Hinn said:

> In Cincinnati, the Lord spoke to me – and He just said the words again. He told me, 'I am going to anoint the people tonight to receive power over demons' ... Before you leave this stadium tonight, every person here will receive a fresh flowing of God's power on your life, and you are going to see demons bow when you say, 'in the name of Jesus Christ of Nazareth'. It has never happened before, but in a few minutes from now, every person here or at home is going to receive that anointing power over demons. Many people will be slain by the power of the Spirit by watching this tonight, and literally thousands upon thousands are going to receive power over Satan. We are going to bury the devil.

Hinn would claim that his words were fulfilled but not all would agree with his claim!

## d) Spiritual help

An example of a revelation involving spiritual help is cited by James (*The Varieties of Religious Experience*, 1960, page 396), in his chapter on Mysticism:

One day in orison [prayer], on the steps of the choir of the Dominican church, he [Saint Ignatius] saw in a distinct manner the plan of divine wisdom in the creation of the world. On another occasion, during a procession, his spirit was ravished in God, and it was given him to contemplate, in a form and images fitted to the weak understanding of a dweller on earth, the deep mystery of the holy Trinity.

# 4 The difficulties in assessing their truth value

As was noted above, one of the features of revelatory experiences is the subject's sense of certainty. It is this type of experience in particular that is inclined to be mistrusted.

The Catholic Church subjects alleged revelations to rigorous tests. Tests include the agreement of the revelations with the teachings of the Church, and the integrity and state of spirituality of the recipient. (For further discussion on this see Chapter 9, page 92.) Only after 13 years of examination by a commission comprised of clergy, physicians and scientists did the Catholic Church pronounce the Fatima apparitions as worthy of belief on 13 October 1930. Some would still question their authenticity.

This mistrust of revelations from God is nothing new. Teresa of Avila wrote that 'even if alleged revelations fulfil the criteria of agreement with Scripture and of increasing the soul's tranquillity, confidence, and devotion to God, if they are important, require action, or involve another person, then a wise confessor should be consulted'.

Franks Davis ( *The Evidential Force of Religious Experience*, page 41) notes that this reservation about revelatory experiences can be found in other religions. She cites Buddhism, where the monk Mettanando Bhikkhu cautions that the insights which mediators think they obtain are more often wrong than not. The requirement is that the subject must have reached a very advanced stage of meditation and that the insights must be shared by other meditators of high rank.

## Answering questions on Chapter 6

By the end of this chapter you should understand what is meant by 'revelation' and be able to explain the difference between propositional and non-propositional revelation. In addition you should be able to illustrate and comment on the main features of revelation. The difficulties in assessing the validity of such experiences should be able to be critically evaluated.

An exam question might be *Explain the different types of religious experience.*

This requires discussion about the major types of experience such as visions, mysticism and revelation. Good answers would include appropriate exemplification.

The first section in this chapter referred to the claimed revelations at Fatima. On 13 May 2000 Pope John Paul II gave details of the third secret. It is interpreted as a prophetic message – a vision of a struggle between the Church and a totalitarian system – and culminates in a vision of an assassination attempt on the Pope (a man 'clothed in white' who 'falls to the ground apparently dead, under a burst of gunfire').

At the release of the text Cardinal Joseph Ratzinger (now the new Pope Benedict XVI) reiterated the Vatican line that the secret referred to events that had already happened. The cardinal said that, after the 1981 assassination attempt by Turkish gunman Mehmet Ali Agca, 'it appeared evident to his Holiness that it was a motherly hand which guided the bullets past, enabling the dying Pope to halt at the threshold of death'. In other words he saw himself as the person referred to in the prophecy. Also the prophecy was seen to have been fulfilled in the successive events of 1989, which led, both in the Soviet Union and in a number of countries of Eastern Europe, to the fall of the Communist regime which promoted atheism. For this too the Pope offered heartfelt thanks to the Virgin Mary. For the full text and the Vatican commentary see web page: *http://www.ewtn.com/fatima/apparitions/Third_Secret/Fatima.htm*

The material in this chapter is useful when discussing the role and importance of religious experiences; in particular the section on faith, religious practice and religious founders in Chapter 11 (pages 106–111).

# 7 Near-death Experiences

## 1 What is a near-death experience?

What would you list as the great questions that still remain unanswered? Is there life on other planets? What is consciousness? Judging by the interest in **near-death experiences** (NDEs), one question that continues to intrigue people is 'What happens after death?' The website *www.nderf.org* hears daily from people who give accounts of their claimed NDEs. Dr Long, who runs the website, gives the research definition of an NDE as 'a lucid experience associated with perceived consciousness apart from the body occurring at the time of actual or threatened imminent death'.

In one sense, NDEs are a particular form of out-of-the-body experience (OBE). Both have the characteristic of the subject observing things from a point located outside their physical body. However in Celia Green's book (*Out-of-the-Body Experiences*, 1968), which is a detailed analysis of claimed OBEs, there is no clear religious or spiritual element in the accounts. In contrast, the accounts of NDEs consistently speak of meeting a 'being' of light and the experience often has a great spiritual effect on the person having the NDE. Fenwick (*The Truth in the Light*, 1995) argues that the NDE has similar characteristics to mystical experiences.

### a) A common experience

In 1943 in Texas, a 21-year-old US army private, George Ritchie, was pronounced dead from double pneumonia. After about nine minutes an orderly noticed the hand of the 'corpse' move and adrenaline was pumped into Ritchie's heart. He made a full recovery and recounted his experiences of this time. Dr Raymond Moody, a lecturer at the University of North Carolina, met Ritchie some years later and on hearing of another similar account began to search for others. As a result he published a collection of 150 accounts and coined the term

Bosch's *Ascent into the Empyean*

'near-death experience'. His book (*Life after Life*, 1975) became an immediate best seller.

Accounts of similar experiences can be traced from early times. Carol Zaleski (*Otherworld Journeys*, 1987) identifies a wealth of similar stories from diverse sources such as Zoroastian eschatological traditions, Islamic traditions, the Dialogues of Gregory the Great and even Plato and his account of a soldier named Er who leaves his body and journeys (*The Republic*).

Equally the nineteenth and twentieth centuries, prior to Moody's book, saw a spate of literature about deathbed visions. These were fed both by interest in spiritualism and by medical and psychiatric studies of response to the threat of death, which were forerunners of the hospice movement.

One study was by Albert Heim, a Swiss geologist, who himself had an NDE when he fell in the Alps. He collected accounts from other Alpine climbers who had survived serious falls. Heim presented his findings in 1892, concluding that 95% of his cases had similar subjective experiences. In 1961 Karlis Osis analysed more than 600 questionnaires that doctors and nurses returned detailing the experiences of dying patients. He found that about 10% experienced vivid visions. Interestingly, he also found that some of the accounts were of frightening sensations.

Ten years later, Russell Noyes, Professor of Psychiatry at the University of Iowa, studied a large number of accounts and saw in them recurrent patterns. What Moody achieved was to make claims of NDEs known to a much wider range of people.

The book gave rise to much debate and a flurry of medical research into the claims. Many assumed Moody was exaggerating, but he claimed in response that no one had noticed the experiences before because the patients were too frightened to talk about them. Dr Sabom dismissed the whole business as nonsense but when challenged to carry out a systematic study in two hospitals at the University of Florida, was amazed to find his results agreed with Moody's accounts and made him reconsider the relationship between mind and brain. The similarity of the accounts by people who claimed an NDE so impressed Dr Kenneth Ring that he too carried out a detailed study and again agreed with Moody on the main features of the 'core experience'. The movement gathered momentum so that in 1978 the main researchers had joined together to form the Association for the Scientific Study of Near-Death Phenomena. This group has a website *www.iands.org* and is now known as the International Association for Near-Death Studies (IANDS). In 1982, a Gallup poll found that about one in seven adult Americans had been close to death and about one in 20 had claimed an NDE.

A recent study was published on 15 December 2001, in the international medical journal *The Lancet*. It was a 13-year study of NDEs observed in ten different Dutch hospitals and looked at 344 patients who were successfully resuscitated after suffering cardiac arrest. Rather than using data from people reporting past NDEs, researchers talked to patients within a week of suffering clinical death and being resuscitated. (Clinical death was defined as a period of unconsciousness caused by insufficient blood supply to the brain.) About 18% of the patients in the study reported being able to recall some portion of what happened when they were clinically dead, and 8–12% reported going through 'near-death' experiences, such as seeing lights at the end of tunnels, or being able to speak to dead relatives or friends.

In 2003, Dr Bruce Greyson published an article (*General Hospital Psychiatry* 25:269–76), in which he describes a three-year study of 1595 patients hospitalised in a cardiac care unit – 10% of patients with cardiac arrest and 1% of patients with other heart problems had NDEs.

## b) The main features

What convinced many people about NDEs was the common experience or 'core experience' that subjects related. Various attempts have been made to list the features of these experiences. Moody himself identified fifteen that described a 'complete' experience, though he was not claiming that all fifteen occurred in every NDE. The list comprises:

- Ineffability
- Hearing the news
- Feelings of peace and quiet
- The noise
- The dark tunnel
- Out of the body
- Meeting others
- The being of light

- The review
- The border or limit
- Coming back
- Telling others
- Effects on lives
- New views of death
- Corroboration.

In contrast, Ring listed five 'stages': peace, body separation, entering the darkness (tunnel), seeing the light, and entering the light. He found that the later stages were reached by fewer people, which seems to imply that there is an ordered set of experiences waiting to unfold.

In 1995, Fenwick detailed a study of over 300 NDEs in his book *The Truth in the Light*. He lists twelve features, admitting that the events described don't always occur in the same order, and few people experience every event:

- Feelings of peace
- Out of body
- Into the tunnel
- Approaching the light
- The being of light
- The barrier

- Another country
- Meeting relatives
- The life review
- The point of decision
- The return
- The aftermath.

Read the following accounts of NDEs and see how many features you can identify.

> My fear vanished. I saw a distant light that was friendly and warm, and felt myself drawn towards it. There was just a feeling of tremendous peace. I felt I was floating, weightless, I appeared to see only a tunnel. I think I looked down on myself in bed, but this was very brief. There was a light or glow at the end of the tunnel, a beautiful gold like the sun rising. I felt it was warm and pleasant. It made me feel very secure and loved. I saw someone, but no one I knew. He held out his arms to me, he was smiling and called my name. I seemed to know what he was saying but he didn't appear to talk to me. It was more a sort of telepathy. I felt very comfortable and secure. At the time I felt it was Christ. There was no evil,

> nothing frightening. I reached out to touch his hands, but he told me I was not ready to join him and I must go back and I would recover. I knew I had only to touch his hands and I would join him. There was definitely some threshold I had to cross. At the time I thought it was betwixt Heaven and Earth. I felt reluctant to go. I felt I had experienced something wonderful.
>
> (*The Truth in the Light*, pages 39–40)
>
> I went down what seemed like a cylindrical tunnel with a bright warm inviting light at the end. I seemed to be travelling at quite a speed, but I was happy, no pain, just peace. At the end was a beautiful open field, a wonderful summery smell of flowers. There was a bench seat on the right where my Grampi sat (he had been dead seven years). I sat next to him. He asked me how I was and the family … He said he was worried about my son; my son needed his mother, he was too young to be left. I didn't want to go back, I wanted to stay with him … I honestly believe in what happened, that there is life after death. After my experience I am not afraid of death as I was before my illness.
>
> (*The Truth in the Light*, pages 35–6)

# 2 Is it a religious experience?

## a) A mystic experience?

Certainly some of the key features of a mystical experience occur in near-death accounts. For example Fenwick comments that the NDE subject 'feels that he has seen through the very texture of the universe into its ultimate structure' (page 17). Also the NDE shares some of the characteristics of a mystic experience such as an intense realness, ineffability, transcendence of space and time, feelings of joy and peace, and positive changes in attitude and behaviour.

In addition, the 'radiant and glowing' figure at the end of the tunnel experience is often associated in the mind of the subject with a spiritual being such as God or Jesus or Allah.

## b) Occurrences in world religions

The appearance of 'otherworld journey' narratives occurs in most cultures and in the traditions of a number of world religions. Indeed such experiences may have been the source of belief in life after death for many cultures. Mircea Eliade (*Mythologies of Death*, 1977) suggests that some ideas about life after death may have originated in Shamanistic trances as these recount the Shaman leaving his body.

## i) Christianity

An often-quoted example from Christianity is in the New Testament:

> I know a man in Christ who fourteen years ago was caught up to the third heaven. Whether it was in the body or out of the body I do not know – God knows. And I know that this man – whether in the body or apart from the body I do not know, but God knows – was caught up to paradise. He heard inexpressible things ...
>
> (2 Corinthians 12:2–4)

The out-of-body experience and vision of paradise recounted by Paul both feature in modern NDEs.

An account from Gregory the Great (a sixth-century Pope) in his *Dialogues*, tells the story of a soldier who died and was revived:

> He said there was a bridge, under which ran a black, gloomy river which breathed forth an intolerably foul-smelling vapour. But across the bridge there were delightful meadows carpeted with green grass and sweet smelling flowers. The meadows seemed to be meeting places for people clothed in white ... In that place each one had his own separate dwelling, filled with magnificent light.
>
> (Dialogues 4:38)

## ii) Tibetan Book of the Dead

There are some close parallels between modern accounts of the near-death experience and the *Bardo Thodol* (The Tibetan Book of the Dead). This scripture from the Mahayana tradition of Tibetan Buddhism was traditionally read aloud to the dying to help them attain liberation.

> O nobly-born, when thy body and mind were separating, thou must have experienced a glimpse of the Pure Truth, subtle, sparkling, bright dazzling, glorious, and radiantly awesome, in appearance like a mirage moving across a landscape in spring-time in one continuous stream of vibrations.
>
> (Bardo Thodol)

The scripture speaks of seeing the pure and immutable light of Amida Buddha. However it also states that:

> The Dharmakaya (the Divine being) of clear light will appear in whatever shape will benefit all beings.

This is consistent with the argument of those who say that cross-cultural differences are merely about the interpretation that is appropriate to the occasion. Hence when AJ Ayer, the atheist philosopher, had a near-death experience, he spoke in terms of being 'aware that this light was responsible for the government of the Universe'.

## iii) Pure Land Buddhism

Paul Badham (*Religious and Near-Death Experience in Relation to Belief in a Future Life*, 1997) identifies a number of parallels between modern NDEs and features in the Sukavativyuha-sutra, including the land beyond described as a wonderful garden with flowers of intense vividness of colour, of bright jewels and of the air vibrant with celestial harmonies.

# 3 Is the near-death experience real?

> **KEY QUESTION** Does the near-death experience provide evidence for life after death?

For many experiencers, the near-death event seems unquestionably to provide evidence for life after death. By contrast, for many scientists these experiences are just hallucinations produced by the dying brain and therefore of little interest.

## a) The implications

If the accounts of NDEs are of true events, then the implications are quite far reaching.

As regards our religious understanding, it has been claimed that these experiences show evidence for:

- life after death;
- soul–body dualism;
- a spiritual realm/presence, indicated by the 'figures of light';
- judgement – a review of life is often cited as part of the experience.

As regards our ethical views, it has been claimed that these experiences influence attitudes towards euthanasia. The peace and joy that accompany these experiences have led many to a positive attitude towards death and dying. Karlis Osis (*At the Hour of Death*, 1977, page 2) comments:

> These experiences are transformative. They bring with them serenity, peace, elation, and religious emotions. The patients die a 'good death' in strange contrast to the usual gloom and misery commonly expected before expiration.

## b) Reasons to doubt the experience

Besides accounting for the experiences by means of natural explanations (see next section), there are some general points that make people question the validity of NDEs:

## i) Lack of objectivity of interviewer

Moody (*Reflections of Life after Life*, 1977) acknowledged that any interview technique is 'flawed scientifically since ... questions convey information'. Because of the nature of the experience, the encounter between subject and interviewer is unlikely to be emotionally neutral and therefore the interviewer cannot help but influence the way in which the subject comes to terms with their experience. Also, the interviewer can unconsciously steer the conversation through the use of subliminal signals just as much as by overt body language and direct speech.

A related problem is the fact that NDE descriptions are so well known that it is difficult to know how much people's accounts of experiences are influenced by this familiarity.

## ii) Cross-cultural differences

In 1986 Pasricha and Stevenson (*Journal of Nervous and Mental Diseases*, Volume 174) carried out a study comparing the components of NDEs from India and America. They noticed some significant differences. For instance the cases from India described being taken by messengers and meeting a man with a book.

The idea of stigmata was also prevalent in the Indian accounts. While the Western accounts referred to feelings of joy and peace, these were absent from the Indian accounts.

## iii) Medieval differences

Medieval accounts have very differing characteristics to modern-day accounts. The tunnel experience seems to be absent and instead a guide would take the person to the next world by varying means including sailing in a ship or treading a bright carpet.

A major feature of medieval experiences researched by Carol Zaleski (*Otherworld Journeys*, 1987, pages 65–9) involved a test bridge over a fiery river. This seems to have been replaced in modern accounts with crossing a border, which suggests that the whole experience is imagination. Surely if there was only one type of existence after death all experiences of that life would coincide.

## iv) **Monism** not **dualism**

Much present-day understanding rejects a dualistic view of human beings. The idea that the mind can be separated from the physical body or that the mind can function when the brain is dead is dismissed given that the mind is seen as a function of the brain. Likewise many would deny the concept of a spiritual realm.

Pause at this stage to think about the points just raised. How might NDE believers reply to them? Check your ideas against some of those given at the end of this chapter.

## c) Natural explanations

A wealth of material has been written on how to assess the NDE in terms of neurochemistry, physiology and psychology. In general, the focus has been on the various individual elements of the experience rather than to give one explanation for the whole event. To say that the experience is nothing but imagination or a hallucination does not explain the various features that seem a core to NDEs. Hence there are various theories that seek to account for specific features.

### i) Moment of death

There is much debate about what constitutes death, and particularly the moment of death. Our definition of death changes from cardiac failure to brain wave cessation as medical science progresses. Many would question the notion of 'a moment of death' but prefer to speak of 'a process of death'. As a result, the claim by subjects that they have 'died' could be false. Indeed the sheer anecdotal nature of many of the accounts means near-death lacks scientific scrutiny and they lend themselves to wrong diagnosis such as errors in EEG readings (these measure the electrical impulse in the brain which reflects the brain's activity). Hence the experiences cannot convey what happens after death, if the person was not really dead.

### ii) Drugs

The fact that the subject is usually a patient in hospital and on medication allows for the chemicals in the body to be the cause of the experience. It is well known that drugs can produce visionary experiences. The tunnel experience does not only occur near death. It is also experienced in epilepsy and migraine, or when falling asleep, meditating or just relaxing, or where there is pressure on both eyeballs, and with certain drugs, such as LSD, psilocybin and mescaline. Aerial perspectives and a sense of leaving the body are common in drugged states, argues Ronald Siegel (*The Psychology of Life after Death*, 1980).

### iii) Oxygen deprivation

In 1980, a neurologist named Ernst Rodin analysed his own NDE and concluded it was a 'toxic psychosis' induced by an oxygen starvation of his brain. The feelings of bliss, the mistaken belief he was dead and his sense of timelessness, he attributed to hypoxia (*The Journal of Nervous and Mental Diseases*, Volume 168). This loss of oxygen also triggers seizure activity in the brain's limbic system. Since the 1930s and William Penfield's work with epileptic patients, it has been known that such seizures produce panoramic recall which could account for the element of sudden and unsought life review. The **temporal lobe** of the brain is involved with the synthesis of emotion and is particularly sensitive to lack of oxygen. It is argued that when this part of the brain is deprived of oxygen it generates the strong feelings of emotion that are elements of the NDE.

A recent theory, again involving lack of oxygen, has been proposed by Tom Troscianko and Sue Blackmore (*Journal of Near-Death Studies*, 1989). Oxygen deprivation increases electrical noise in the visual cortex. In normal circumstances there are lots of cells representing the centre of the visual field but very few for the edges. However when electrical noise is increased the pattern changes and the centre begins to look like a white blob and the outer edges gradually get more and more dots. And so it expands until eventually the whole screen is filled with light. The appearance is just like a dark speckly tunnel with a white light at the end, and the light grows bigger and bigger (or nearer and nearer). This could be interpreted by the brain as moving through a tunnel towards a light.

## iv) Endorphins
Discovered in the early 1970s, endorphins are morphine-like chemicals secreted by certain brain cells during extreme stress. They block some of the effects of trauma and shock. Some would claim that this results in a near-death vision.

## v) Sensory deprivation
According to Ronald Siegel, the brain turns inwards in search of substitutes for its sensory nourishment, and it is this that creates the near-death vision. For instance, he argues that the sense of going through a tunnel towards a bright light 'is the result of stimulation of the central nervous system that mimics the effect of light on the retina' (*The Psychology of Life after Death*, page 923).

## vi) Birth
Carl Sagan made popular the explanation that the sensation of moving down the tunnel was really a birth experience. He argued that at the point of death the memory of birth is re-lived and hence the tunnel is likened to the birth canal. The white light is the light of the world into which you were born and even the being of light can be 'explained' as an attendant at the birth.

## vii) Memory model
This explanation seeks to account for the view of floating above and looking down. The mind constructs a model of reality. Our senses create the best and most stable model. However, when you are almost asleep, very frightened or nearly dying, the model from the senses will be confused and unstable. If you are under terrible stress or suffering oxygen deprivation, then all the models will be unstable. The biological system will then try to reconstruct reality from memory – possibly the memory of being in hospital. When it does this it may

be that the mind creates a bird's-eye view. The events or scenes are seen as though from above.

Whatever we can imagine clearly enough will seem real. But what will we imagine when we know we are dying? It is likely that many people will imagine the world they expect or hope to see. Their minds may turn to people they have known who have died before them or to the world they hope to enter next. This could also account for the experience of the other world and seeing people we know. The apparent accurate description that some give about their surroundings and of being resuscitated may be the result of effects of the treatment they are receiving and hearing what is going on. Hearing is the last sense to be lost and you can imagine a very clear visual image when you can only hear something. So the dying person might build up a fairly accurate picture in this way.

### viii) Coping strategy
NDEs could be our response to the threat of impending death. The brain creates a fantasy to persuade us that death is not the end, but the beginning of some new and exciting existence.

### ix) ESP
In a sense this can be seen as supporting NDEs as it implies the mind has an ability to go outside the body. However some have argued that if ESP exists then this would explain any information that the subject conveys that was not attainable by normal means. Hugh Montefiore (*The Paranormal – A Bishop Investigates*, 2002) cites a case where a woman in Harborview Hospital, Seattle, reported seeing a tennis shoe lying on a window ledge on the third floor of the hospital. The shoe was only found after a search and could not be seen from inside the building. If ESP exists then there is no need to believe there is evidence of life after death, just extrasensory perception before death.

Pause at this stage to think about the points just raised. How might NDE believers reply to them? Check your ideas against some of those given in the next section.

## d) Conclusions

Needless to say, these natural explanations have not gone unchallenged. Those supporting the validity of the NDE argue that:

### i) Natural explanations are inadequate
- If drugs were an adequate explanation, then how do we account for those who had no medication at all or where, despite differences in the types of drugs administered to the patient, people had the same core experience?
- If the explanation is oxygen deprivation, then why are the memories so orderly and clear?

- The re-birth explanation is said to be flawed since babies do not have the brain facilities to store memories of birth, nor is the brain developed enough in a newborn baby to be able to perceive objects. In addition, the baby does not have the sensation of moving towards the light as their face is pressed against the wall of the birth canal. Also the theory predicts that people born by Caesarean section should not have the same tunnel experiences. Sue Blackmore (*Birth and the OBE*, 1982) conducted a survey of people born normally and those born by Caesarean (190 and 36 people, respectively). Almost exactly equal percentages of both groups had had tunnel experiences (36%).
- Near-death reports do not conform to individual or socially conditioned expectations. Osis and Haraldsson (*At the Hour of Death*, 1977) cite cases where the experience conflicts with the subject's professed desires, fears or beliefs. Hence it cannot be explained as a wish fulfilment.
- Although ESP may explain some events, it does not explain how people meet relatives in the 'afterlife' even when they were unaware those relatives had died. Children who have had an NDE are particularly good examples, since they describe vivid events, people and places with words and knowledge that are beyond their years. They do not expect to die and they have not been exposed to cultural or religious views, yet their accounts match the elements of the common core.

### ii) Other features not explained

- As was shown in Section 1 (page 61), the experience is world-wide. There seems to be no correlation between the content of the experience and such factors as age, gender, medical condition, medication, religious beliefs or knowledge of near-death literature.
- One of the most noticeable features of the NDE is the transforming effects it produces on the person. There was a loss of a fear of death that stayed with them years later. Also, people claim that they are no longer so motivated by greed and material achievement but are more concerned about other people and their needs.
- The research published in *The Lancet* (see Section 1, page 62) concluded 'Our results show that medical factors cannot account for the occurrence of NDE'. The scientists were surprised that those who had experienced an NDE recalled their experience with the same degree of detail when interviewed again several years later.

Clearly there is a great deal of difference in opinion in the whole area of NDEs which may make it near impossible to reach a decisive conclusion.

## Answering questions on Chapter 7

By the end of this chapter you should understand what is meant by a near-death experience and be able to discuss and illustrate some of the main features from a variety of sources. You should also be able to critically assess the validity of the experience.

This topic lends itself to critical evaluation of the validity of the experience. Evaluation at a simple level is commenting about the view presented. That includes reflecting or responding to those arguments and so discussing rather than just listing them. Only by doing this is it possible to demonstrate the evaluative skill. You will then have a conclusion that has been justified by the evidence and argument. In this chapter there are arguments given both for and against regarding the NDE as real. A good critical assessment would consist of a sustained and integrated argument that had systematic reasoning and analysis. A possible exam question would be *Explain the issues that arise in attempting to authenticate near-death experiences, and assess the claim that near-death experiences can never be authenticated.*

It should be noted that in fact this is a two-part question in the sense that the first part is identifying issues, while the second part is evaluating a particular claim.

Some of the issues that might be identified could be the difficulty in weighing up alternative explanations; the problem that different experiences seem to give different concepts of God (divine being), and the subjective nature of the experience means there are problems in verifying the claimed experience.

The second part, involving assessment, could lead to a discussion about what would count as 'proof'. Further debate may include examining who the authentication was for – the one who has the experience or others?

# 8 Triggers of Religious Experiences

## 1 Introduction

It has long been known that certain conditions or environments seem to trigger religious experiences. In more recent times there has been research into the stimulation of the temporal lobes and the monitoring of the effects of certain drugs. This is discussed more fully in Chapter 10. Besides this there appear to be certain other religious rituals or environments, of a more traditional nature, that seem to stimulate religious experience.

There is one notable piece of research into triggers of religious experiences carried out by Greeley (*Sociology of the Paranormal*, 1975). His results are shown in Table 8.1 and will be considered in more detail.

**Table 8.1** Triggers of religious experiences (percentages of those reporting an experience)

| | | | |
|---|---|---|---|
| Listening to music | 49% | Being alone in church | 30% |
| Prayer | 48% | Reading a poem or novel | 21% |
| Beauties of nature (e.g. sunset) | 45% | Childbirth | 20% |
| Quiet reflection | 42% | Sexual activity | 18% |
| Attending services | 41% | Your own creative work | 17% |
| Listening to sermon | 40% | Looking at a painting | 15% |
| Watching children | 34% | Physical exercise | 1% |
| Reading the Bible | 31% | Drugs | 0% |

## 2 Music

Music is used in worship in most religions and is often accompanied by dancing. At the extremes, frenzied drumming and rhythmic dancing, through to modern-day repetition of emotional choruses, reflect the part music sometimes plays in religious worship. Hymns are a way of expressing shared beliefs and generating shared emotions. Spickard (*Experiencing Religious Rituals*, 1991) argued that this shared worship could lead to a special kind of communal experience and social cohesion. Classical sacred music can often stir people's hearts and minds deeply. Music for requiem masses can be particularly powerful.

Dance is often an expression of religious devotion, especially when thankfulness and joy are experienced. Dance can also form part of initiation rites. The best-known dancers associated with religious experience are the whirling dervishes. The main dance consists of circular dancing, whirling and leaping, with each movement symbolising a spiritual reality. One dance involves each dervish spinning round while moving slowly around the room. One hand is raised, pointing to heaven, while the other hand points down to Earth. This symbolises the dervish trying to become a channel of communication between the two. The whirling dervishes are particularly associated with the Sufi tradition of Islam. **Sufism** is the inner, mystical dimension of Islam and is divided into Orders or Brotherhoods. Each Order teaches its own path (tariqah), or method of achieving union with Allah.

In a more unusual context, rhythmic dancing precedes the handling of poisonous snakes, which is practised by the 'Church of God with Signs Following'. The practice of handling snakes is believed to have started with George Hensley in the hills of Tennessee. It is said that during one of Hensley's sermons about Mark 16 (look up verse 18), some men tipped out a box full of rattlesnakes in front of him.

Whirling dervishes

Without flinching Hensley reached down and picked up the snakes, preaching the entire time. By 1914 the practice of handling snakes had spread throughout the Church of God. However, the actual act of snake handling was only practised by a small portion of the members and, because of laws in the USA outlawing this practice, it has now virtually disappeared.

# 3 Prayer

**KEY QUESTION** Does prayer work?

In a 1991 Gallup poll it was found that about 40% of people in Britain and about 60% in the USA pray daily. An old Jesuit saying is 'Prayer is the soul's lifeline to God', and James described prayer as 'the very soul and essence of religion'. There are various types of prayer. Using Christianity as an example, seven different types can be identified that occur in the Bible:

- Blessing (Ephesians 1:3)
- Adoration (Psalms 95:6)
- Petition (Colossians 4:12)
- Asking forgiveness (Luke 18:13)
- Intercession (1 Timothy 2:1)
- Thanksgiving (1 Thessalonians 5:18)
- Praise (Ephesians 3:20).

In a sense all religious experience is about prayer, i.e. communion with God. This section focuses on the commonest type of prayer, petitionary or intercessory, i.e. asking for help for oneself or others. This is just one small part of prayer for those who are committed to spiritual practice. Many who are deeply committed to a religious faith may well spend much time each day in prayer, whereas some people, in contrast, pray just as a last resort.

With prayer, as with all religious experiences, there are problems of verification. Most Christians believe prayer is real and valid. It is impossible to prove that during prayer, communion with God takes place, unless one accepts the premise that God exists and wants us to pray. Whether you believe the premise to be true depends on whether or not there is evidence for God or religious faith. Is it possible for there to be any kind of evidence, even in theory, that God answers prayer? Maybe there could be an experiment where a group of people pray quite specifically for some things that are very unlikely to happen. If, over a period of time, a very large number of things they prayed for occurred so frequently that it was unlikely to be coincidental, then it might be claimed that there was some evidence that God answered prayer.

Some have attempted such an experiment. In 1959, for example, Loehr carried out a prayer experiment on plants. Some seeds received prayer for growth, others for no growth and still others received no prayer at all. He claimed that those that received prayer for growth showed a higher germination rate and more growth.

Other studies have included experiments in prayer therapy. In this test, 45 volunteers with neurotic and psychosomatic disorders were divided into three groups. One of the groups was prayed for over a period, one group was not prayed for and one group was randomly prayed for. The prayer therapy group was claimed to have shown a 72% improvement in both symptoms and test results. Such experiments continue, for example *The God Experiment* by Russell Stannard. Despite these attempts at proof, scepticism remains and proof is elusive.

What criticisms would you make of such experiments? Check the section at the end of the chapter for some ideas.

In Lecture 19 (*The Varieties of Religious Experience*), James cites the case of George Muller of Bristol (1805–1898) as an example of a prayerful life. Muller established five large orphanages as well as distributing millions of copies of religious material. He had only two shillings (10 pence) in his pocket when he decided to embark on his orphanage work. Without making his wants known to anyone, he prayed about his needs and received gifts of over £1,400,000 for the building and maintaining of these orphanages. James refers to Muller's prayers as '… of the crassest petitional order. Early in life he resolved on taking certain Bible promises in literal sincerity, and on letting himself be fed, not by his own worldly foresight, but by the Lord's hand' (page 447). Pierson's biography of Muller (*George Muller of Bristol: His Life of Prayer and Faith,* 1899) gives numerous examples of how prayer was seemingly answered. For instance, there was the occasion when it was time for breakfast but they had no food for the children in the orphanage. Muller prayed, 'Dear Father, we thank Thee for what Thou art going to give us to eat'. Immediately they heard a knock at the door. When they opened it, there stood the local baker who said that he couldn't sleep and somehow felt he had to get up and bake bread for the orphanage. Soon, a second knock was heard. It was the milkman. His cart had broken down in front of the orphanage. He said he would give the children the milk so he could empty the cart and repair it.

In keeping with Muller's experiences, William Temple, a famous Archbishop and theologian of the twentieth century, said, 'When I pray, coincidences happen, and when I don't, they don't'.

In Christianity, one of the focuses of the Pentecostal churches has been on speaking in tongues, particularly when praying. Speaking in tongues is claimed to be the New Testament phenomenon where a person or persons speak in a language that is unknown to them. The Pentecostal experience may be defined as seeking and receiving the gift of speaking in tongues as a sign of the Baptism of the Holy Spirit. Kildahl (*The Psychology of Speaking in Tongues*, 1972, page 2f) gives an example of how speaking in tongues (**glossolalia**) can be initiated:

> Typically after an ordinary evening church service, interested members of the congregation are invited to remain in church in order to discuss the gift of tongues. The leader encourages the people to 'receive' this ability going from one another laying his hands on each person's head. 'Say after me what I say, and then go on speaking in the tongue that the Lord will give you'. One might utter a few syllables, speak for two or three minutes, or ten, or not for several days and while at home. 'It was the best I ever felt in all my thirty-one years' … Once possessed of this ability, a person retains it and can speak with fluency whenever they choose. It is referred to as a 'direct and personal encounter with the Holy Spirit'.

Within Christianity, many traditionalists are uneasy about some of the claims of the Charismatic Movement to such religious experience. Some challenge it on theological grounds, claiming that the gift of tongues was only given in the Early Church times and then ceased. Others challenge on grounds that what we see being exhibited today is not the same as speaking in tongues in the New Testament, and that natural explanations can explain today's phenomenon. It has been claimed that glossolalia has a specific language structure based on the language tongue of the speaker; that the linguistic organisation is limited; and that the capacity to speak in this type of semi-organised language can be duplicated under experimental conditions. Thus, on this view, glossolalia does not appear to be a 'strange language', but rather the aborted or incomplete formation of familiar language. In contrast, others claim it is the work of the Holy Spirit, reviving and equipping the Church with a new outpouring of the Spirit.

# 4 Meditation

One of the goals of meditation is to obtain a religious experience. The theistic religions seek union with God, while non-theistic religions such as Buddhism seek the loss of self.

## i) Theistic

In some ways it is difficult to make a clear distinction between prayer and meditation. These, in turn, are closely linked to mysticism. For instance Teresa of Avila distinguishes between four states of prayer:

- the prayer of quiet (a form of meditation)
- the prayer of union
- the state of ecstasy
- spiritual marriage (feeling of oneness with God – mystical union).

St Bonaventure (1221–1274) made a similar connection. He saw prayer/meditation as a preparation for a mystic experience. He divided the experience into three stages:

- the purgative stage (the mystic is purified and prepared for the experience through meditation)
- the illuminative stage (the mystic is illuminated both cognitively and emotionally)
- the unitive stage (the mystic gains a continuing union with the Divine).

### ii) Non-theistic

James (*The Varieties of Religious Experience*, page 386) says that in India, the training in mystical insight is yoga. He defines yoga as 'the experimental union of the individual with the divine'. By means of exercise based on such things as diet, posture, breathing and intellectual concentration, the person seeks to enter the condition termed 'samadhi'.

> ... the mind has a higher state of existence, beyond reason, a superconscious state, ... then this knowledge beyond reasoning comes ... There is no feeling of *I*, and yet the mind, works desireless, free from restlessness, objectless, bodiless. Then the Truth shines in its full effulgence, and we know ourselves ...

> (cited by James, page 386)

There has been much research into yoga and meditation generally in terms of examining the physiological effects of these practices. There is evidence of reduction in heart rate, blood pressure and anxiety, and some changes in brain rhythms. Other techniques aim to increase the breathing and almost hyperventilate. For a good survey and discussion on experiments on meditation see pages 172–184 in *Psychology of Religion*, by David Wulff (1991).

## 5 Mantras and religious symbols

Another aid to reach these states is the chanting of mantras. Mantras are words or phrases that are chanted out loud or internally as objects of meditation. In Buddhism, these mantras are often associated with particular Buddhist figures, whose qualities can be cultivated by the repetition of the relevant mantra. Equally the recitation of verses is a way of cultivating an awareness of the qualities of the Buddha (Buddhanusati). As we saw on page 54, Guru Nanak was given a mantra. In other religions, the focus could be on nature or a religious picture, or a religious symbol. Such images are seen as a window into an eternal realm.

Check what the following religious symbols represent in the section on answering exam questions at the end of the chapter.

# 6 Deprivation

Deprivation is an aspect of asceticism. **Asceticism** is the suppression of the body for spiritual ends. It reflects a dualistic view of body and spirit. The Greeks believed that the human body is inferior and corrupting, but that only the spirit is pure. They believed that the body must be suppressed if the spiritual plane was to be reached.

## a) Sensory

In most religious traditions, there has been a long history of holy men living in isolation in the desert or in small caves. Muhammad sought solitude in the desert to feel nearer to God, John the Baptist is described as a prophet preaching in the wilderness and Jesus is said to have gone into the wilderness for 40 days. In addition, various accounts in the Bible identify mountains as places where God can be met (e.g. Moses, Elijah). Religious followers have taken up this concept of isolation.

In the Christian tradition, those who seek solitude are known by a variety of names such as hermits (from the Greek word for 'desert'), anchorites (from the Greek word for 'withdrawal') and monks (from the Greek word for 'solitary'). Those who sought isolation in the desert became known as the Desert Fathers, the most well known being Anthony. In 270 CE, when Anthony was 20 years old, he felt a call to a life of prayer and reputedly lived in the desert until he died at the age of 105. He spent vast amounts of time in prayer and meditation, often denying himself food or sleep for long periods, and claimed to have had various visitations from angels as well as demons. In contrast, the anchorites often volunteered to live in a cell attached to a church. A typical cell would be about 12 square metres. Often it would have one window, which gave a view towards the choir where the mass could be heard and communion received, and on the opposite side another window where food was received. Usually these volunteers were male but there were also females (anchoresses), one such being Julian of Norwich.

A less extreme modern example of the seeking of quietness is the religious retreats of many Christian churches and the Ashrams of the Hindus.

## b) Sleep

As an act of devotion, many religious followers elect to go without sleep to keep some form of vigil. In other cases lack of sleep is one aspect of ascetic discipline. William James cites a passage from the autobiography of Saint Teresa, in which she refers to Saint Peter of Alcantara:

> Saint Peter [of Alcantara] had passed forty years without ever sleeping more than an hour and a half a day. ... To compass it, he kept always on his knees or on his feet. The little sleep he allowed nature to take was snatched in a sitting posture, his head leaning against a piece of wood fixed in the wall. Even if he wished to lie down, it would have been impossible, because his cell was only four feet and a half long.
>
> (cited by James, page 350).

The effects of sleep deprivation are well documented and include delusions, hallucinations and disorientation. Many cults have been accused of depriving its members of sleep so as to be able to brainwash them.

## c) Food

Fasting is one of the Five Pillars of Islam. Muslims practice *sawm*, or fasting, for the entire month of Ramadan. This means that they may eat or drink nothing, including water, from sunrise to sunset. Likewise, the Jews have a prescribed fast on the Day of Atonement. In contrast, the Christian tradition has no compulsory fasts. One of the purposes of fasting is to take our eyes off the things of this world and instead focus on God. A good discussion of the physiological and psychological effects is given by Wulff (*Psychology of Religion*, 1991, pages 63–66).

# 7 Ritual

Often prayer and fasting are preparation for certain ritual actions, ceremonies or festivals.

Momen (*The Phenomenon of Religion*, 1999, page 105) claims that 'Ritual is probably the most common source of religious experience for the majority of people'. Others describe ritual as 'the choreography of the soul'. Momen lists the numerous forms of ritual. It is worth noting that millions of Muslims take part in prayer five times a day, following a cycle of ritual postures, and millions of Christians take part each week, or even daily, in the ritual of the Holy Communion service (variously known as the Mass, Eucharist or Lord's Supper).

Pause and consider what types of ritual there are and check your ideas with those listed in the section on answering exam questions, at the end of this chapter.

# 8 Corporate acts of worship

As has been noted (Section 2), shared worship can lead to a special kind of communal experience. Durkheim (1915) held the view that the origin of religion lay in 'collective effervescence', that is, intense emotional arousal that strengthened social bonds. Ritual also reinforces this communal experience. It gives a feeling of group solidarity and unity and a sense of belonging to something that is greater than the individuals who comprise it. The reading and preaching of the sacred text can also be the trigger for religious experience. For instance, Muslims, Hindus and Christians all consider their scriptures as the revealed word of God. Through these texts and others, God speaks to the individual.

# 9 Holy people

Some religious leaders or spiritual people have been seen as the source of a religious experience for others. In Hinduism, 'sadhu' is the name given to the holy men of India. Believers only have to behold a sadhu to receive a spark of his spiritual energy. They give donations to the sadhus, regarding the donation as an offering to the gods, and in return receive a blessing.

# 10 Holy places

Holy places can be seen as a trigger for religious experience. Usually they are places where either something happened or people feel something sacred, possibly worship having taken place there for a great length of time, e.g. Makkah or the Sikh Golden Temple at Amritsar. Often they become places of pilgrimage like Lourdes or the sacred river Ganges. Such locations are seen as places where there is a sacred meeting between the spiritual and the physical. The temple in Jerusalem in Isaiah's vision (Isaiah 6) is seen as a replica of something in heaven.

## Answering questions on Chapter 8

By the end of this chapter you should be able to identify, illustrate and explain a number of possible triggers of religious experiences.

This chapter also contains useful material when answering questions on the role and importance of religious experience (Chapter 11). Prayer is mentioned on some exam specifications as another type of religious experience. In this chapter only petitionary prayer has been discussed. You need to add to this list so that you can explain and comment on the other types of prayer listed on page 75.

The symbols shown on page 79 are:

- Hindu symbol – the Sanskrit letters for the holy sound 'Om'. Om is the primordial sound, the first breath of creation, the vibration that ensures existence. The Om sign signifies God, Creation and the One-ness of all creation
- Christian symbol – the symbol of the crucifixion and the price Jesus paid for the salvation of all people. Symbol of hope, love and sacrifice
- Buddhist symbol – there are various forms of mandalas with distinct concepts. Each detail has symbolic meaning. The purpose of the Mandala is concerned with the process of invocation, the calling in and realisation of the spiritual force within the meditator themselves.

Momen (*The Phenomenon of Religion*, page 105) identifies various forms of ritual: rites of purification, regeneration, thanksgiving, self-denial, penance and propitiation. They are often rites of passage, rites related to the calendar or the formal re-enactment of a sacred story or event.

# 9 An Argument for God's Existence

## 1 Religious experience and God

**KEY QUESTION** Can religious experience show that God probably exists?

As we shall see in this chapter, there have been various approaches to using religious experience to show the likelihood of God's existence. It is an important issue as to whether God exists. Many claim that they have had experiences in which they apprehend a divine reality. Are those who never experience such things missing out? Or are those who claim the experience deluded? In this chapter, the arguments for God's existence using religious experience will be examined. In Chapter 10, the contribution of physiology and psychology to this debate will be discussed.

## 2 Philosophical arguments

An argument can be defined as 'a set of statements, which is such that one of them (the conclusion) is supported or implied by the others (the premises)'. For example:

All Chinese eat noodles.
Joseph is Chinese.
Therefore Joseph eats noodles.

The first two statements are the premises, and the third is the conclusion. Philosophers distinguish between two types of argument. The example above is a deductive argument because the conclusion necessarily follows from the premises. If the premises are true then you would have to agree with the conclusion.

If philosophy only considered this type of argument then disputes between philosophers would be rare, and fewer philosophy books would be written. However there is another type of argument, the inductive. This form of argument is less persuasive but much more common, for example:

All Chinese eat noodles.
Joseph eats noodles.
Therefore Joseph is Chinese.

Can you work out how this is different from the deductive argument?

Can you explain why the conclusion does not necessarily follow from the premises even if the premises are true?

The problem with **inductive arguments** is their obvious limitation of always being open to doubt and uncertainty. These arguments are more conclusions in terms of degrees of persuasiveness. In the strict philosophical sense for an argument to be a proof it has to be a valid deductive argument and the premises must be known to be true. The arguments for the existence of God are of the inductive type (except perhaps for some forms of the ontological argument) and this might explain why God's existence continues to be debated.

It should also be noted that something that is convincing to one person often carries no weight with another. We need to be conscious of the various presuppositions that each of us holds, and how these affect the way we interpret the evidence.

## 3 Three approaches using religious experience to show the likelihood of God's existence

This argument has featured in Western philosophy where the concept of God has been classical **monotheism**.

### a) Inductive argument

The design argument looks at features of the universe and infers that the best way to account for them is an appeal to the existence of a God. One form of the religious experience argument works in a similar way. It considers subjective accounts of experiences that have a particular characteristic, and then, like the design argument, infers that they can only be adequately explained in terms of divine agency – God.

The logical form can be expressed in various ways using premises and conclusion, for example:

- P1 If an entity is experienced then it must exist.
- P2 People claim they experience God.
- Therefore God probably exists,

Richard Swinburne

This form of argument is an inductive argument. Remember that in an inductive argument the conclusion may follow from the premises but it does not necessarily follow. Hence this argument can never be considered a proof but may be persuasive.

Richard Swinburne (*Is there a God?*, 1996) points out that it is reasonable to believe that God would seek to interact with his creatures and he gives a list of examples such as God telling us things individually to provide us with a vocation or to authenticate a revelation which we need. God loves us and so may simply show himself to particular individuals. However many might regard alternative explanations to these experiences as more probable than concluding that such an entity as God exists.

## b) Cumulative argument

Many regard the different arguments for God's existence as being finely balanced and not decisive either way. Indeed, Swinburne (*The Existence of God*, 1979, pages 290–1) argues that 'the probability of theism is none too close to 1 or 0'. He then considers the religious experience argument and sees this as making theism overall probable. Swinburne argues that his conditions have been met as regards his two principles of credulity and testimony (see Section 5 below), and having shown that the other theistic arguments cannot be classed as 'very improbable' he concludes that theism is more probable than not.

The usual **cumulative argument** takes the form of accepting that though each argument in itself is not a proof, the arguments, when added together, become more convincing. In other words, theism is the one solution that all the arguments point to and that most satisfactorily takes account of the wide range of data. Various analogies have been used to illustrate this approach. For instance, if you have a leaky bucket (inductive argument for God's existence) and insert other leaky buckets inside it (more arguments for God's existence), then the leaks are sealed (i.e. the arguments gain strength).

Can you see any criticisms to this approach?

Variations of cumulative arguments often appeal to Occam's razor, which claims that unnecessary entities should be erased. Hence the solution to all the questions raised by the theistic arguments, such as cause, order, regularity, morality and religious experience, is the one entity, called God. This is regarded as a simpler solution since it only requires the single entity 'God'.

Can you think why some people may not regard 'God' as a simpler solution?

## c) Direct awareness of God

This approach does not focus on a reasoned argument – in fact it has no actual argument at all. Experience gives a direct way of knowing about things, distinct from the indirect, inferential way provided by reasoning. Perceiving Victoria Station is the best way of knowing it exists.

It rests on the view that belief in God is reasonable, not because its truth is entailed by the conclusion of a series of premises, but because God can somehow be directly encountered or immediately perceived. In philosophical jargon this is called a foundational or basic belief, in the sense that such beliefs are not derived from any other belief. An example of an agreed foundational, basic belief is 'I am in pain'. I know it is true, not by reasoning from other beliefs, but by direct experience.

Alston (*Perceiving God*, 1991) drew attention to the fact that in reports of religious experience, God is experienced as having various qualities, for example, good, powerful or loving. As a result, some doubt has been cast on whether it is correct to describe these as foundational beliefs. Is it not necessary for some inference to have taken place to arrive at such conclusions about God? Everitt gives an example to clarify this view:

> I look at Fred and thereby acquire the belief that Fred is good. How is this belief to be justified? On the assumption that I am not actually witnessing Fred do or say anything which is good, the justification must surely refer (a) to Fred's visible appearance, and (b) to some correlation

between people having that sort of appearance and their being good. In other words, the justification of the belief requires some inference.

(*The Non-existence of God*, 2004, page 154)

# 4 A veridical experience?

When considering the argument from religious experience, it is important to clarify what elements are necessary for the experience to be categorised as 'an experience of God'. As we saw in Chapter 2, religious experiences are very wide ranging. Consider the following:

> As Saul neared Damascus on his journey, suddenly a light from heaven flashed around him. He fell to the ground and heard a voice say to him, 'Saul, Saul, why do you persecute me?'

(*Acts* 9:3–4)

> I was filled full of an everlasting sureness that took hold of me in power without any dread ...

(Julian of Norwich)

Can you see how these two accounts of a religious experience differ?

The first involves the senses (seeing and hearing) while the second does not involve any of the five senses. Many religious experiences involve both a sensory and a non-sensory aspect, with the non-sensory aspect being regarded as the more important feature. With regard to the argument from religious experience, whether the experience was sensory or non-sensory, it would seem necessary to believe through reason that the source of the experience is an objective mind-independent God who is revealing itself to the person. In other words the entity God exists, whether the perceiver exists or not. Such a religious experience is called a **veridical** experience.

If such veridical experiences occurred then God's existence would necessarily follow. So the heart of the argument involves demonstrating that the religious experience is veridical. As Everitt comments:

> She will need to argue to the occurrence of [veridical] religious experience before she can argue from it.

(*The Non-existence of God*, 2004, page 156)

It is this very issue that Richard Swinburne has addressed with his Principle of Credulity and Principle of Testimony.

# 5 The Principle of Credulity and the Principle of Testimony

Swinburne's argument is focused on the onus of proof and put in the context of ordinary sense experiences. He argues that we are justified in accepting that an event occurs unless there are strong reasons to the contrary, for example reasons for supposing the viewer was hallucinating! It is up to the disbeliever to show that it is unreasonable to believe the account, rather than for the believer to show that it is reasonable to believe. In other words it is a case of religious experiences being viewed as true until proven otherwise.

This principle can be expressed formally as: 'In the absence of any special considerations, if it seems that X is present to a person, then probably X is present'. What one seems to perceive is probably the case. Swinburne points out that unless we do this we cannot know anything. We would have to be sceptical about all our sense experiences. If my experience of seeing a cat in a tree does not justify my belief that there is a cat in the tree – then it seems that I could never be justified in believing that there is a cat in the tree. Nor indeed anything else for that matter.

Swinburne then lists four considerations that, if present, would cast doubt on the reliability of the account:

- If subject 'S' was unreliable.
- If similar perceptions are shown to be false.
- If there is no strong evidence that X was not present.
- If X can be accounted for in other ways.

However, he feels that these four considerations do not weigh against religious experience. For example:

- if the person is known to be a liar – but this does not account for all cases
- if the experience itself was made under circumstances that have proved unreliable in the past – for example, if the person is under the influence of LSD. Again this does not account for all cases!
- given God is everywhere, the opposer according to Swinburne would need to show that God did not exist. This they have not done
- it can be accounted for in other ways – but to find the causal chain in my brain, such as, for example, the temporal lobes, does not show that it is unreliable. God is everywhere and sustains all causal processes, therefore He can use normal means to communicate with me.

If you want to read a full account of this, then see Chapter 13 in his book *The Existence of God.*

Swinburne's second principle is the Principle of Testimony. He argues that, in the absence of special considerations, it is reasonable to believe that the experiences of others are probably as they report them. In other words we should believe other people unless we have good reason not to. Clearly he accepts the point that people can lie or be mistaken, but the significance of this approach is to put the onus on the sceptic to show that religious experience should be rejected rather than for the believer to show that it is true. This approach may not show that any religious experiences are veridical, but equally it does show that they could be. This is particularly important as a cumulative argument if all the other arguments for the existence of God are evenly balanced.

# 6 The case against

Swinburne used the ordinary sense experience as a parallel to a religious experience. However it is questionable whether it can be authenticated in the way that an ordinary sense experience can. Religious experiences are very much a private matter rather than public and it is not possible therefore to check someone's religious experience. A number of points have been discussed about this whole area.

## a) Is an 'experience of God' a philosophically sound notion?

When people try to describe an experience of God, they tend to make comparisons that raise problems of philosophy. Analogies are appealed to, to justify the philosophical notion of a religious experience of God, but many argue that the analogies have weaknesses:

- It is like a sense experience: people argue that just as you can encounter a table, you can also encounter God, but the two are very different. For instance, God is not material, nor does He have a definite location. Also claims can be checked of encounters with objects, but when the object is God, they are not checkable.
- It is similar to an experience of people: people argue that just as we are known to each other by a kind of direct apprehension rather than through our physical body, so in the same way we experience God who is non-corporeal.
- Can God be recognised? The problem arises as to how you can distinguish God from other possible objects of experience. For instance God is said to be Creator. How would you recognise that attribute? God is said also to be omnipresent, infinite, omnipotent and eternal. But how, simply by virtue of an awareness of an object or experience, can anything be recognised to be that? To recognise omniscience, you would have to be omniscient yourself! James reaches a similar conclusion: 'I feel bound to say that religious experience ... cannot be cited as unequivocally supporting the infinitist belief. The only thing that it unequivocally testifies to is that we can experience union with something larger than ourselves ...' (*The Varieties of Religious Experience*, page 499). Indeed the argument has been extended to claim that none of God's properties is perceptible, for God is not the sort of being who has an appearance that could be presented in experience. In other words all religious experiences can be classified as 'special considerations' according to Swinburne's Principle of Credulity. Everitt

(*The Non-existence of God*, page 174) gives a helpful illustration. If someone said they were perceiving the square root of 2, then the principle of credulity could not be applied since the square root of 2 is not a perceptible object. Hence the belief about the experience must be wrong.

- Direct experience of God is impossible: some claim that the finite cannot experience the infinite, so we cannot experience God. Others argue that to speak of a direct experience is not philosophically correct since we infer and interpret every experience. For instance even an ordinary object is mediated and interpreted via our sense data and organs. Indeed it could be argued that the religious person interprets according to a religious framework of life, while the atheist interprets as purely natural events. Hick referred to this as 'experiencing-as' and illustrated it using the ambiguous figure of the 'rabbit-duck'.

How do you think believers may reply to each of the criticisms made above? It is important in evaluation not just to cite the criticism but to respond to it and try to weigh up how effective it is. Some possible responses to these criticisms are listed at the end of this chapter on page 94.

## b) There is a natural explanation

The fourth of Swinburne's special considerations was that the experience could be accounted for in other ways. Many people question the religious reality behind the experience and suggest there are natural explanations but the person has misinterpreted it. These areas will be discussed at length in Chapter 10. However, in outline they are listed below.

### i) The physiological

Drugs do seem to be linked to religious experiences in that, for example, the Aztecs are known to have used a drug. Likewise marihuana is used in parts of the West Indies by such groups as the Rastafarians, as was LSD amongst some religious groups in the USA in the 1960s.

A test carried out on theological students during a Good Friday meditation (1966) involved half being given a drug and half a placebo. The result was that those on drugs had significantly more religious experiences. Such evidence implies religious experiences have a physiological explanation. Appeals to the existence of a religious gene and the role of the temporal lobes in causing such experiences have been the latest focuses of research.

### ii) The psychological

The part the mind plays in causing supposed religious experiences has long been debated. Some see conversion as meeting the psychological needs of people, while Freud saw religious experience as a reaction to a hostile world. We feel helpless and seek a father figure. Thus we create a God who is able to satisfy our needs.

Other psychological states suggested to account for such experiences include mental illness, sexual frustrations, adolescence and guilt, and particular personality types.

For further discussion on physiological and psychological explanations see Chapter 10.

## c) Reasons that make it unlikely

Some people feel that there is an inconsistency about the argument from religious experience. They say that if the argument were true then surely certain things would be expected to follow. Some examples are given below.

### i) Lack of uniformity of experience
The fact that different experiences are recounted seems to count against the argument. If God were the source of them all, surely there would be greater similarity between them. Some see Allah, some see the Virgin Mary, some see Jesus. Others just experience a great power. Very few (if any) Hindus have visions of the Virgin Mary, and very few (if any) Roman Catholics have visions of Vishnu. If Hinduism is true then Roman Catholicism is false and vice versa.

In reply it might be argued that:

- different experiences are not logically incompatible. Indeed scholars like James argue for a vague general similarity in the experiences
- God reveals himself in terms of cultural beliefs that we will understand and interpret
- the fact that different experiences recounted does not mean that they are therefore all in error. It could be argued that only one religion is correct so the other religious experiences are false, but those of that one religion are true
- the lack of uniformity may also be due to the interpretation rather than the falsity of the actual religious experience
- the fact that different world religions report religious experiences may imply that all religions are equal and valid and all roads lead to the same mountain top – they just happen to take different paths.

### ii) Not all experience it
If God existed, He would want everyone to know about Him and therefore all should have religious experiences. However:

- perhaps some precondition, like faith, is required. God is hidden and ambiguous, so we have to enact our freedom. Moral and

spiritual goals have value only if the agent is free to pursue or not to pursue them. Indeed believers assume often that others can have the experience and even encourage them to do so (for example, evangelism)
* the initiative may have to come from God, who may be selective
* perhaps He does reveal Himself but we are unable to see it. Just as a blind person cannot have the same experience as a sighted person, so it may be that those who do not have religious experiences lack spiritual 'sight'.

### iii) There is no God, therefore the experience of God cannot be valid
If God existed, the experiences must have a naturalistic explanation. This is an *a priori* conviction, whose reasons would need to be examined. However, this approach has gained strength in recent times with the debate about whether God is really an object/being. Some reject the traditional understanding of the word 'God' and see it more as a 'form of life' that the believer inhabits. It is a way of expressing a particular way of looking at the world and does not refer to any external objective being.

## 7 Are there any tests to apply?

Religious experience is not a conclusive argument for the existence of God. One may believe that what is experienced is actually God, but there is always the possibility that others may interpret it differently.

Whether religious experience is seen to be caused by God will depend to a great extent upon individual presuppositions. If our presuppositions favour particular types of experiences we are more likely to be convinced of reports of them.

### a) Criteria that would add weight to validity
* The experience must be in keeping with the character of God as made known in different ways, for example through natural theology, agreement with doctrine, resemblance of experience to classic cases in religious tradition as judged by spiritual authorities.
* The results of the experience should make a noticeable difference to the religious life of the person. It should lead to a new life marked by virtues such as wisdom, humility and goodness of life. It should build up the community rather than destroy it. Teresa of Avila said:

Though the devil can give some pleasures – only God produced experiences leave the soul in peace and tranquillity and devotion to God.

* The person should be regarded as someone who is mentally and psychologically well-balanced.

Wainwright (*Philosophy of Religion*, 1988) comments that the only conclusive grounds for rejecting religious experiences would be:

- proofs of the non-existence of God and other supernatural entities
- good reasons for thinking that the perceptual claims immediately based on these experiences are inconsistent
- evidence that the experiences are produced by natural mechanisms known to systematically cause false beliefs and delusive experiences.

Wainwright's personal conclusion is that so far, critics have not provided these grounds. For a very different conclusion read Chapter 10 in Mackie's book *The Miracle of Theism* (1982).

It should also be noted that some argue that the origin of an experience is irrelevant. The fact that the source may be an ordinary experience doesn't mean that the experience can't become a religious one by the interpretation of the subject.

# 8 'If I experienced it, then I would believe'

If an experience happens to you personally it may change your perception of what is true. If it happens to someone else, it is less likely to change your perception, even if you accept that the experience has happened and that logically proves the existence of an outside force (God).

There are at least three levels of assessment:

- What actually do I think happened?
- How do I interpret it?
- Would I interpret it differently if the experience had happened to me rather than to someone else?

People often say 'Well I would have believed it, if it had happened to me'. Why is that?

I think it is to do with the way we assess things. We like to think we are objective, analytical and coldly logical. However, we are not dealing just with facts when we assess truth and our interpretation of the event (if it really did happen); we reach conclusions that involve some intuition. When it happens to us, we can't divorce ourselves from it. Of course we must be aware of wishful thinking, and so on, and people will take such things into account to differing degrees.

We do assess experiences closer to home differently. For example, the death of a parent or child may cause us to lose faith, whereas the death of someone way outside our immediate circle of family or friends may have little influence on our thinking or faith. That isn't wrong or necessarily inaccurate. Indeed the person having the experience has a more accurate picture since it happened to them, and telling others with words that don't really convey adds to the weakness for others. The experience affects us in a way that just recounting to others can't affect them. It doesn't mean our assessment is wrong.

Intuition asks – given the totality of the data presented to us by our experience of life, does it make better sense in the light of the God hypothesis? Does it all hang together better if we assume there is a God?

## Answering questions on Chapter 9

By the end of this chapter you should understand the difference between deductive and inductive arguments and be able to express, in a philosophical form, the religious experience argument for the existence of God. In addition, you should be able to critically evaluate the religious experience argument. Remember that some aspects of the debate are discussed more fully in the following chapter.

A possible exam question would be: *To what extent can religious experience be viewed as a reasonable argument for the existence of God?*

Remember that there are various forms of the religious experience argument for God's existence. Avoid any discussions of types of experience. This is a common fault where candidates start writing at length about mysticism, etc. Some philosophical terminology would be expected such as 'inductive argument' as well as some key thinkers, such as Richard Swinburne. Reasonableness often involves risking a hypothesis as true in the light of other competing statements, as well as weighing up the probability of the evidence. However, the failure to find a more probable competing hypothesis does not prove that there is none. Equally, there remains the difficulty over how we individually weigh up what is more probable. This in turn is affected by our presuppositions.

Did you work out how the illustration of the inductive argument differs from the deductive (page 84)? The conclusion may follow from the premises but it does not necessarily follow. For instance, Joseph may be English but love eating noodles. In this case the premises would still be true but the conclusion would be false. Just because all Chinese eat noodles this does not exclude other people also eating noodles.

The criticisms against the cumulative argument centre around the point that a failed argument, added to another failed argument, results in both failing (i.e. $0 + 0 = 0$). Others have questioned the assumption that there is a paradigm standard of rationality. For further on this see my book, *Philosophy of Religion*, in the same series as this one.

Many would also challenge the view that the positing of 'God' is a simpler answer, given the complexities surrounding the concept of God and the apparent contradictions in his nature (for example, the problem of evil).

The integrating of arguments such that you weigh one against another in juxtaposition requires you to know responses to a view. The type of responses you could make to the arguments given in Section 6a (page 89) include questioning whether the assumption is correct that people are non-corporeal (i.e. dualistic nature). Even if people are mind and body, we still encounter them when they have bodies. Knowing they are there, involves knowing that their bodies exist. In contrast God has no body at all. Therefore an encounter with God is radically different from an encounter with a person. In addition, we are aware of how many people we are having an encounter with, i.e. they are physical units distinguishable in some way from others, because it involves reference to material factors. However, when we encounter God, he is not material, yet is said to be one being.

Another debate centres around whether God could be recognised. One solution is to argue that an experience of God would be a self-authenticating experience. However, feelings of certainty can occur when in fact I am wrong. Just declaring that 'You know' is insufficient. There must be reasons as well as convictions.

The illustration using the square root of 2 (page 90) has been challenged by Alston. He uses a counter-illustration of a coloured object, arguing that modern science has shown us that colour is not an objective property of objects, yet we perceive it. So even if God does not possess perceptible properties, there is no reason why he should not appear to possess them. It has also been questioned whether the properties such as omnipotence and omniscience are not perceivable. The claim that such properties cannot be perceived begs the question against those who claim that they have perceived.

# 10 Physiological and Psychological Perspectives

## 1 Introduction

Apparent conflicts between religion and science are not new. In 1650 Bishop James Ussher calculated that the Earth was created in 4004 BCE on Saturday 22 October at 8 a.m. (A calculation based on the literal interpretation of Genesis.)

A more recent conflict has centred around the theory of evolution. Darwin's theory was seen by many to destroy the credibility of Christianity. Alister McGrath (*The Twilight of Atheism*, 2004) suggests that this crisis of faith in Victorian England came about because of a particular concept that people had about God. This concept had partly been formed through William Paley's book about the design argument. He had written *Natural Theology* in 1802 and had tried to counter some attacks on the arguments for God's existence.

Paley's argument was based on design for a specific purpose and used the watch analogy. It argued that nature was a mechanism and hence intelligently designed. God created all things good and hence they required no modifications. Darwin's theory of natural selection portrayed nature as a battleground and undermined the watchmaker image!

The argument still continues, as is illustrated by the writings of Richard Dawkins. His recent works such as *The Blind Watchmaker* (1986) and *A Devil's Chaplain* (2003) reflect the clash as he sees it between religion and science. He claims 'Science is free of the main vice of religion, which is faith'. In a recent book (*Dawkins' God: Genes, Memes and the Meaning of Life*, 2004), Alister McGrath, a theologian and a scientist, strongly challenges Richard Dawkins' case.

In recent times, besides developments in the field of physiology, two new disciplines have come into conflict with religion – **psychology** and **sociology**. All of these have offered explanations of religious experience and in doing so raised questions about the cause and validity of such phenomena. For instance, many argue that the consistency of spiritual experiences across cultures, across time and across faiths suggests a common core that is a likely reflection of structures and processes in the human brain. The **atheistic** philosopher AJ Ayer concluded that:

> The mystic does not give us any information about the external world, he merely gives us indirect information about the condition of his own mind.

Bertrand Russell put it more starkly:

> From a scientific point of view we can make no distinction between the man who eats little and sees heaven, and the man who drinks much and sees snakes.

The last chapter (page 90) pointed to some of these 'natural' explanations to religious experience and these will now be examined.

# 2 Physiological perspectives

> **KEY QUESTION** Do claimed religious experiences have a natural explanation?

Physiology is the branch of the biological sciences dealing with the functioning of organisms.

## a) Drugs

The effect of drugs on religious experience has been suspected for a long time. Known usage of drugs in a religious context includes the Aztecs using mescaline and the Rastafarians using marihuana. The main psychoactive drugs associated with religious experience research are the hallucinogens, mescaline, psilocybin and LSD. Because of modern laws about use of drugs, recent research has been curtailed.

William James wrote about his own experiences (*The Varieties of Religious Experience*) in his chapter on mysticism. He claimed to have undergone a religious experience with nitrous oxide that made him aware of 'forms of consciousness entirely different' (page 374).

- Probably the best-known piece of research was done by Pahnke in 1962. He used as a basis Stace's list of mystic experience characteristics to enable him to decide whether a subject had had a religious experience. To be counted as a mystical experience it was decided that both the total score and the score in each separate category must be at least 60–70%. Twenty theological students from relatively similar religious and socio-economic backgrounds were selected. Half were given a psilocybin pill, half were given a placebo. They then listened over loud-speakers to a meditative Good Friday service in a private basement chapel while the actual service was in progress in the church above. The drugs were administered double-blind, so that neither the experimenter nor the participants knew the specific contents of any capsule. When all the data were analysed, the scores of psilocybin subjects were higher to a statistically significant degree in all categories than those of the control subjects. In regard to degree of completeness, only three or four of the ten psilocybin subjects reached the 60–70% level of completeness, whereas none of the control subjects did.

- Another series of experiments was carried out at the Massachusetts Mental Health Center during 1965 and 1966. Forty older professionals were selected. This time seven out of 20 of the experimental group and one out of 20 of the control group reported mystical experiences. In contrast Masters and Houston (1966) found only 3% reported mystical experiences in their testing of 206 subjects with LSD.

Can you think of any criticisms of this research on drugs? Check the Answering Questions section at the end of this chapter.

## b) Temporal lobes

For many years it has been known that the **temporal lobe**, when stimulated, produces altered perception. A lot of the early work was done with sufferers of temporal lobe epilepsy. This condition consists of having seizures centred around intense electrical activity in the temporal lobes. Some report that during seizures they have profound religious experiences. VS Ramachandran describes this:

> ... most remarkable of all are those patients who have deeply moving spiritual experiences, including a feeling of divine presence and the sense that they are in direct communication with God. Everything around them is imbued with cosmic significance. They may say, 'I finally understand what it's all about. This is the moment I've been waiting for all my life. Suddenly it all makes sense.' Or, 'Finally I have insight into the true nature of the cosmos.' ... God has vouchsafed for us 'normal' people only occasional glimpses of a deeper truth ... but these patients enjoy the unique privilege of gazing directly into God's eyes every time they have a seizure.

> (*Phantoms in the Brain*, 1998, page 179)

- Wilder Penfield, a neurosurgeon, worked with patients who suffered epileptic fits. He conducted a series of stimulation experiments with 1100 patients over a number of years (*The Mystery of the Mind*, 1975). When he stimulated the right temporal lobe with a mild electrical current, his patients reported hearing voices and also experiencing features similar to those reported by people who had had an NDE. Similar links to religious experience were found by Dewhurst and Beard in 1970, who reported that out of 69 patients

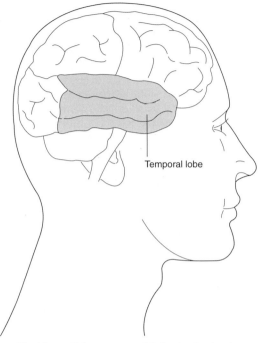

Position of the temporal lobe in the brain

with temporal lobe epilepsy, 26 showed an interest in religion after the onset of epilepsy compared with only eight previously.
- Spectral imaging techniques have enabled researchers to show that certain regions of the brain are active during various types of religious experience. For example, the frontal lobe is active during times of intense meditative concentration, while the middle temporal lobe is linked to emotional aspects of experience (such as joy and awe). A region in the parietal lobe goes dark when subjects experience a sense of unity with the universe. Some researchers think that this part of the brain governs the sense of self in time and space and the concentration prevents the brain from distinguishing between self and not-self. Hence an impression of being one with the universe.
- In the 1980s, Dr Persinger designed a helmet that produced a safe stimulation of the temporal lobe. He claimed that it produces an experience in over 80% of test subjects, who report feeling a 'sensed presence'. Persinger's view is to see religious experience as nothing more than a pathological reaction to adverse stimuli. 'The God Experience is an artifact of transient changes in the temporal lobe' (*Neuropsychological Bases of God Beliefs*, 1987). He argues that it is the context that interprets the experience as religious.

Can you think of any criticisms of this research? Check the Answering Questions section at the end of the chapter.

## c) Genes

Most researchers think it unlikely that there will be a single gene for religious activity, but there is some evidence that there is some sort of genetic component. Several studies of identical twins separated at birth and brought up separately have claimed to measure religiosity (defined as the intensity of religious belief).

- Recent findings by a research team led by Laura Koeing at the University of Minnesota suggest that as adolescents grow into adults, genetic factors become more important in determining how religious a person is. The twins in the study (169 pairs of genetically identical twins and 104 pairs of fraternal twins, all male) believed that when they were younger all of their family members shared similar religious behaviour. However in adulthood, only the identical twins reported maintaining that similarity. In contrast, the fraternal twins were about a third less similar than they were as children. Some have argued that some basic features of personality may have been inherited that are associated with religiousness.

Can you think how believers might reply to this theory? Check the Answering Questions section at the end of the chapter.

## d) External deprivation

Isolation and sensory deprivation are claimed to be significant factors in explaining religious experiences of holy men living in some sort of wilderness. Using a sensory deprivation tank, Hood and Morris (*Journal for the Scientific Study of Religion* 14, 1981) reported that sensory isolation, combined with a religious suggestion, produces religious experiences in those who are high in intrinsic religiosity. One explanation for this, given by Michael Argyle (*The Psychological Perspective on Religious Experience*, 1997), is that the left-brain hemisphere is quietened so that messages from or mediated by the right hemisphere are more dominant.

Can you think of any criticisms of this research? Check the Answering Questions section at the end of the chapter.

For discussions on internal deprivation involving self-esteem, and so on, see the section below.

## 3 Psychological perspectives

Psychology is the science of human thought and behaviour. Given that roughly one person in three claims to have had a religious experience, researchers have investigated whether there is any correlation between such things as personality types and religiousness.

## a) Demographic variations

In a survey carried out by Hay (*Religious Experience Today*, 1990), he found that:

- women report more religious experiences than men
- religious experiences gradually increase with age
- educated individuals are more active in aspects of religion and report more religious experiences
- incidences are higher amongst upper middle class than unskilled workers
- they occur in members of all denominations and none, and also to agnostics/atheists
- occurrences are higher amongst church members.

## b) Personality traits

The most used research-testing method is the Myers–Briggs Type Indicator. This shows that feeling rather than thinking is typical of the religious. Although there seems no difference on extroversion–introversion, in testing, the religious scored higher in the intuitive trait than the sensing trait. Sensors perceive more concretely, while intuitors perceive more symbolically and as part of a larger picture.

## c) Schizotypy

The nature of schizophrenia, and other forms of psychosis, is still under debate and a significant issue is the relationship between psychosis and the mystical, or religious, experience. Schizotypy is a disposition to develop schizophrenia but at a lower level is associated with religious experience and creativity. The term was coined by Claridge in 1985 (*Origins of Mental Illness*) and he argued that there was a correlation between people who had this trait of 'cognitive openness' and those who had a religious experience.

## d) Jung and the human psyche

Jung's location of the source of religious experience is the psyche. He claimed that the psyche consists of various systems including the personal unconscious. However there is a deeper, more significant layer of the unconscious, which he called the collective unconscious. The personal unconscious is made up of contents that have at one time been conscious, but which have disappeared from consciousness through loss of memory or repression. In contrast, the collective unconscious have never been conscious, and owe their existence exclusively to heredity. It is the reservoir of our experiences as a species, a kind of knowledge we are all born with. It influences all of our experiences and behaviours. It is made up essentially of archetypes. They are the ancient, unconscious source of much that we think, do and say as human beings. They form the core of our psychological makeup.

The mother archetype is a classic example of the collective unconscious. All of our ancestors had mothers and they were necessary for our survival. The mother archetype is our built-in ability or principle of maternal care, sympathy and fertility. The mother archetype is symbolised by 'Mother Earth' of mythology, by Eve and Mary in Western traditions, and by symbols such as the Church. According to Jung, someone whose own mother failed to satisfy the demands of the archetype may well be one that spends his or her life seeking comfort in the Church, or in meditating upon the figure of Mary. Jung saw a religious experience as an indirect encounter with the archetypes, and religions as revealing aspects of the unconscious and a symbolic way of interpreting the life of the psyche.

## e) Peak experiences

Maslow (*Motivation and Personality*, 1970) proposed that when lower needs had been satisfied, some people had a further need for self-actualisation. Lower needs included things such as social and esteem needs. One of the characteristics of such people was what Maslow referred to as 'peak experiences'. Peak experiences are sudden feelings of intense happiness and well-being, and include a wider sense of awareness, as though one was standing upon a mountaintop. The experience fills the individual with wonder and awe and so has the characteristics of a religious experience.

## f) Anti-institutionalisation

Some people see the religious experiences of the Charismatic Movement characterised by the 'outpouring of the Holy Spirit' as a social movement struggling against the forces of institutionalisation. For instance the 'Toronto Blessing' allows a freedom where all manifestations of behaviour are accepted or even encouraged. This is a liberation from the restrictions that society imposes upon us.

## 4 Conversion experiences

There are a variety of theories that claim to explain conversion experiences. The growth of new religious movements (NRMs) has provided a particular focus of study about conversion. However this has resulted in some studies seeing conversion as a deviance against a background of 'cults' and 'de-programming'.

## a) Social influence

Such things as the skills of orators, their relationship with those being influenced, and the relations with groups holding the old and new beliefs, are all factors that can influence our attitudes and beliefs. Almost without exception, changing to a new religious orientation takes place through what the sociologists call kinship and friendship networks of one sort or another. People who convert or change religions usually do so through personal contact. Some research also claims that those converted tend to be more socially isolated and this means that individuals are detached from structures that would channel them into conventional activities, leaving them open to new ideas.

Crude emotional manipulation is cited as another explanation for 'conversions'. This could include emotional religious meetings that hype the audience up almost to a frenzy of excitement and expectation, or play on people's vulnerability and fears.

Developmental psychologists highlight the need of the adolescent to explain and systematise. Religion offers this on an overall scale.

## b) Personal crises

William James viewed these as the cause of conversion, and the work of Batson (*Religion and the Individual*, 1993) has developed this understanding. In this view, conversion can be seen as creative problem solving. Often the subject has some dissatisfaction with themselves or is searching for a meaning in life. Low self-esteem is a common feature. Adolescence is the most common period for religious conversions. Usually it involves a personal re-commitment to the common religious tradition rather than a change to a different tradition. After the age of 30 conversions are rare, and surprisingly, on this theory, the 'midlife crisis' does not mark a time of conversion, nor does divorce.

## c) Relationships

It has long been noted that many conversions take place at the age of puberty and some have therefore tried to identify some connection between the two. For instance, either as a form of independence and rebellion against parents or as some form of sexual love.

Freud argued that it was related to the relationship with the father. God is a projected father-figure who is needed as a source of protection but is also a source of fear and guilt. Research claims that converts have had weaker relations with their fathers than matched unconverted people. However, even if people have need for a father-figure, it does not mean that God is not like that. There does still remain the possibility that such a state is a necessary requirement for the experience, but such a state would not necessarily negate a claimed experience of God.

## 5 The effects of religious experiences

Michael Argyle (*Psychology and Religion*, 2000) lists a number of effects, both immediate and long-lasting:

- positive mood, happiness
- altruistic attitudes, such as valuing working for social change and to help others but being less concerned with social status and having a highly paid job
- religious life was enhanced and had deeper commitment. Also less fear of death but a sense of mission
- attitudes to the self were more positive. They felt more at one with themselves
- general health improved though the evidence lacked objectivity.

## 6 Conclusions

Validity or non-validity of a religious experience cannot be determined by the fact that there are some natural explanations possible. Natural explanations could explain away the event but the event could still be because of communion with God (or The Absolute). All they do is to shed some light on the different ways that this experience manifests itself. Ultimately we have to look elsewhere for the evidence, e.g. arguments for the existence of God.

Indeed religions are often very guarded about claims to religious experience, because there are often other explanations, as we have seen above, that could explain them. For example, within Christianity, many traditionalists are uneasy about some of the claims to religious experience of the Charismatic Movement. Indeed, historically those who have claimed seeing visions and hearing voices have often been regarded as highly suspect by the mainstream members of the religion. Many religious followers are quite prepared to see that natural explanations are possible for many so-called religious experiences and that it may be impossible to ascertain whether a particular experience is genuinely from God.

### Answering questions on Chapter 10

By the end of this chapter you should be able to critically evaluate the various natural explanations given to account for religious experience. Remember that critically assessing involves explaining and responding to different views and arguments.

Note that aspects of this chapter link to Chapter 4 (Conversion), Chapter 9 (An argument for God's existence) and Chapter 11 (The role and influence of religious experience).

The material in this chapter will be useful for answering exam questions that require you to assess arguments for the authenticity of religious experiences. Remember that evaluation at a simple level is commenting about the view presented. That includes reflecting or responding to those arguments and so discussing rather than just listing them. Only by doing this is it possible to demonstrate the evaluative skill.

The research on drugs (page 97) suggests that religious experiences are merely chemical changes to the brain, rather than any supernatural cause. However, these conclusions have been challenged. For instance, it may be objected that a theological student would obviously have such an experience because of his familiarity with mysticism and religious language. What is not known is whether someone can experience those characteristics without interpreting them in a religious sense. The experiment itself has also been criticised on the grounds that the subjects were in the same room and knew who had been given the psilocybin and who had not. This could affect the outcome.

Research into the temporal lobes (page 98) has suggested that this can give a natural explanation for religious experiences. However, there is no way to determine whether the neurological changes associated with spiritual experience mean that the brain is causing those experiences, or is actually perceiving a spiritual reality. The brain image cannot tell us if there is actually a picture 'out there' or whether we are creating the picture in our own mind. Religious experience may well be compatible with scientific explanation.

It may well be the case that different patterns of brain activity may appear, depending on the particular experience the individual is having (for example, different brain activity when an NDE experienced compared with praying).

Others have argued that stimulating the temporal lobes does not induce the experience but rather facilitates experiences of reality. Just as giving a pair of glasses may enhance the ability to see distant objects, so perhaps stimulating the temporal lobes helps one to perceive God. The former does not cause a person to doubt the existence of distant objects, so why should the latter cause doubt about the existence of God? Again, even if the experience were false, it would not be necessary to conclude that all religious experiences were false.

In a similar way, the research on genes and deprivation (page 100) does not show that the experience is therefore non-veridical. Maybe the faculties of the person having the experience are functioning as they should. If so, a scientific explanation is irrelevant. As with all of these debates, it is difficult to isolate what is the cause and what is the effect.

# 11 The Role and Influence of Religious Experience

## 1 The problem of ineffability

**KEY QUESTION** Can religious experience be a source of faith?

The appeal to religious experience as a source of faith and belief has been attacked on the grounds that religious experience is non-cognitive. **Cognitive statements** are statements that are true or false in the ways that literal statements are true or false. In contrast, **non-cognitive statements** are not open to verification or falsification. One of the characteristics of a mystical experience is ineffability. This implies that no cognitive claim can be based on them and therefore cannot be a source of faith.

Davis (*The Evidential Force of Religious Experience*, page 15f ) cites five reasons why mystics' claims are said to be ineffable:

- *Poetic hyperbole* – such phrases as 'unspeakable bliss' are a way of emphasising the significance, overwhelming emotion and highly unusual nature of the experience. The intensity is highlighted and the expression is of an experience that is beyond the ordinary.
- *Experience not description* – emotions and sensations must be experienced to be understood. There is a great difference between knowing the definition of drunkenness and actually experiencing being drunk. Metaphors and analogies help to convey the experience.
- *All-encompassing* – mystics often seem left with an impression rather than explicit knowledge. Davis quotes a passage from Teresa of Avila's book, *Interior Castle*, in which Teresa describes how she was taken into a room to see a magnificent display of objets d'art set out in such a way that you could see almost all of them as you entered. Although she could not remember them in detail, she recounts how she could remember seeing them as a whole. This she likens to a mystic experience where you are left with the impression of having 'understood everything'. Davis also comments that some are more gifted than others in their ability to articulate their thoughts and experiences.

- *Paradoxical* – the mystic seems to experience contradictions such as God being both personal and impersonal. This makes it difficult to express.
- *Via negativa* – the emphasis is on what God is *not*, drawing attention to God's otherness.

Davis concludes:

> We have shown above that 'cannot be described' should normally not be taken in the strict sense. The mystic's descriptions may not be adequate; they may be inextricably bound up with models and metaphors, and the divine may remain ultimately beyond the grasp of human concepts, but that does not mean that the often eloquent attempts of the mystic to communicate his 'vision' are not intended to give us some indication of an ultimate reality beyond his own personal life.

> *(The Evidential Force of Religious Experience, page 19)*

# 2 Religious experience as a source of faith

## a) The nature of faith

When trying to define faith, most thinkers have juggled with a mixture of will, propositional belief (see Chapter 6, page 53) and trust. Though Aquinas viewed the Christian faith as rational, in that it could be supported and explored by reason, he did not think that reason alone could discover its truths and insights. Divine revelation was also required. McGrath (*Christian Theology: An Introduction*) identifies three components to Martin Luther's (1483–1546) concept of Christian faith:

- Faith has a personal, rather than a purely historical, reference. Belief in the facts, by themselves, is not adequate for true Christian faith.
- Faith concerns trust in the promises of God. Faith is not just about believing something is true but being prepared to act upon that belief.
- Faith unites the believer to Christ. Faith makes both Christ and his benefits – such as forgiveness, justification, and hope – available to the believer (page 129).

On this view, faith seems to include a **belief-in**, as well as a **belief-that**.

## b) Belief-that and belief-in

In everyday speech to say 'I believe something is true' is often taken to mean 'I believe that it is probably true'. However in its more precise sense, the word 'belief' means 'I have a conviction that it is true'.

That conviction is not necessarily there as a result of logical argument. Belief may come about by deductive argument, by inductive argument, by personal experience or even by sheer blind personal acceptance and prejudice.

As argued above, faith seems to include a belief-in, as well as a belief-that. A typical belief-that statement is 'I believe that the Pope is the Head of the Roman Catholic Church'. The statement is making a claim that is objectively true and that something is a fact. We call this propositional belief. A person believes that:

- some state, process or thing exists independently of the actual belief that they exist
- this belief is more likely to be true than any rival or alternative belief
- the likelihood of one statement of belief being true as opposed to another rival statement being untrue depends upon:
  - the greater or more persuasive evidence for it, and
  - the extent to which the statement is consistent with our general perception of what is true
- the statement is true.

What counts as evidence for the belief will depend on the nature of the statement. The belief that there is a table in the room, will be based on the senses. In contrast, historical statements will be evaluated differently.

The essential issue is that such evidence indicates that a particular proposition is more likely to be true than not, and more likely than alternative propositions. These criteria are what we mean when we speak of a rational belief.

Now consider belief-in statements. An example of a belief-in statement would be 'I believe in Jesus', where clearly this usually means more than just belief that Jesus was an historical figure. It also implies trust in Jesus. Belief-in may be contrasted with belief-that, by saying belief-in conveys an attitude of commitment, trust, or loyalty on the part of the believer. This attitude, or psychological stance, forms part of the object of belief-in. It is, however, difficult to see belief-in as a contrast to belief-that as it would be irrational to trust or be loyal to something one did not believe to exist.

Hence personal trust is often seen as an important element of faith. An act of the will is used in deciding and abiding by that choice. Luther used the illustration of a boat:

> The person who does not have faith is like someone who has to cross the sea, but is so frightened that he does not trust the ship. And so he stays where he is, and is never saved, because he will not get on board and cross over.

(cited by McGrath, *Christian Theology: An Introduction*, page 127)

## c) Faith, experience and reason

A distinction is often made between believing something by faith and believing something by reason. Is this distinction valid? After all, faith is acting on what you have good grounds to think or know is true – a leap, but not a leap in the dark, or an irrational step. Often, faith involves weighing the evidence. Basil Mitchell tells a story about the resistance movement. A partisan meets a stranger whom he believes is the secret leader of the Resistance movement. Sometimes the stranger appears to be working against the movement, but the partisan is told that this is all part of the stranger's plan. He continues to believe the stranger. In the same way religious belief continues sometimes when there appears to be evidence against it. The believer weighs the evidence on both sides and assesses what is the most reasonable and consistent overall view. For instance, a Christian has faith in the love of God as shown by the Cross, despite the contrary evidence of suffering in the world. He would claim that such a position of faith was not unreasonable.

Evans ( *Thinking about Faith,* 1985) comments that:

> a faith which evades critical questions is a faith that lacks confidence, which is not truly assured it has found truth

(page 177)

He argues that if God wants us to choose freely to love and obey him then God couldn't make it *irrational* to be a theist.

For many people, the move from a belief-that to a belief-in, is brought about by a personal religious experience. Some examples are given in Chapter 4, Section 2c. Other examples are also given in Chapter 4 where people come into a faith from either no faith or a different faith. Clearly the religious experience of conversion is central.

Other people's religious experience can also be a source of one's own faith. In particular, a revelation that someone claims to have received can be a source of what people believe. For examples of this, look back at Chapter 6.

Another role of religious experience related to faith is that of encouragement or strengthening faith. Paul's religious conversion on the road to Damascus, was referred to by Paul in his writings to encourage others to believe. In evangelistic meetings, believers often give an account ('testimony') of their own conversion and experience of God, to encourage others.

So what is the relationship between faith, experience and reason? It seems that a religious experience can move people into faith. For example they may have a sudden feeling that God is there, and they believe. Equally, faith can lead people into a religious experience. For example, someone who converts may have some sort of religious experience as they worship and pray. However, it is difficult to link all this to evidence/reason for faith because internal and subjective experiences can usually be explained away or rationalised. In other words, religious experience does not, by its nature, provide good objective evidence for the truth of a particular belief. That evidence must be sought elsewhere.

## 3 Religious experience as a source of religious practice

Religious practice includes ritual, religious ceremonies, religious festivals and way of life. We have already seen (Chapter 8) that ritual can be a trigger for religious experience. The correct performance of the ritual is vital, as is the need for purity in order to participate in the ritual. Dr Geaves (*The Sufis of Britain*, 2000) notes that for a Sufi, it is essential to perform the rituals of Islam as if in the presence of Allah, or, at least, with the awareness that Allah sees and knows not only a Muslim's actions but also his intentions. The variety of disciplines that allow the Sufi to remember Allah are taught in the various tariqas (see page 74).

Equally important is the person who leads the ritual. In many forms of Hinduism, only Brahmin descent entitles a person to priestly function.

Rites of passage are where many people encounter religion directly. The main religious rites of passage correspond to the stages of life: birth/naming, becoming adult/initiation, marriage and burial.

Religious practices can also be based around a religious experience. Many festivals are celebrations of a past event that involved a religious experience. For example, during Ramadan, Muslims celebrate the time when the verses of the Qur'an were revealed to the Prophet Muhammad; Wesak or Vesak, also known as Buddha Day, is when Buddhists celebrate the life of the Buddha and his teachings. They remember the night of his enlightenment and his revelations about the nature of death, karma and rebirth, suffering and desire.

## 4 Religious experience as a source of moral behaviour

One of the common themes in a conversion experience is the sense of a new being, a transforming process, a rejection of the old life and a desire for a new purer life.

> Therefore, if anyone is in Christ, he is a new creation; the old has gone, the new has come!
>
> (2 *Corinthians* 5:17)

As a result of this change, a new lifestyle is required.

> Be imitators of God, therefore, ... and live a life of love ... But among
> you there must not be even a hint of sexual immorality, or of any kind
> of impurity, or of greed, because these are improper for God's holy
> people
>
> *(Ephesians 5:1–3)*

All the religions have an ethical standard and a religious experience can bring a person into a faith so that the person now feels those ethical standards have new authority and are to be followed. Also, a religious experience can empower the believer to live this new ethical life.

## 5 Religious experience as a source of the foundation for religious movements

In most religions there is often a central pivotal figure who is linked to the founding of that religion. Usually these figures experience a particularly significant event that marks the start of their ministry. It is a turning point, which is often followed by a period of doubt and reflection in which they prepare themselves for their mission.

For the religious experiences that are linked to the founders of Islam (Muhammad), Buddhism (Gautama) and Sikhism (Guru Nanak), see Chapter 6. Abraham is a foundation figure in Judaism. His call from God to leave Ur and the establishing of the covenant is recorded in Genesis 12.

> The Lord had said to Abram. 'Leave your country, your people and
> your father's household, and go to the land I will show you.
> I will make you into a great nation and I will bless you:
> I will make your name great, and you will be a blessing.
> I will bless those who bless you, and whoever curses you I will curse:
> And all peoples on earth will be blessed through you'.
>
> *(Genesis 12:1–3)*

Other foundation figures have been instrumental in starting movements within a religion. Again, Chapter 4 contains good examples of this, such as Martin Luther (Protestants/Lutherans) and John Wesley (Methodists).

### Answering questions on Chapter 11

By the end of this chapter you should understand the problem of ineffability and the difference between belief-that and belief-in. In addition, you should be able to critically assess the role and importance of religious experience as a source of faith, religious practice, moral behaviour and as the foundation for religious movements.

A possible exam question would be *Explain how religious experience may be a source of faith, and assess the view that believers cannot rely on religious experience alone as a source of faith and practice.*

The first part of the question involves 'explaining' and so is a knowledge-based skill. Various approaches are possible. For instance mysticism can provide insight into divine reality while a conversion experience leads to faith. Some examples/illustrations are needed for a good answer.

To challenge the role and importance of religious experience you will need to discuss whether it is important that all believers have a religious experience. Also, to what extent, if any, is faith dependent on religious experience? The material in Chapters 9 and 10 will be useful in discussing whether believers could rely on religious experience alone as a source of faith and practice. Many would argue for the need to authenticate the religious experience in some way. The role and authority of scripture may be explored as an alternative to religious experience.

# Bibliography

W Alston, *Perceiving God* (Cornell University Press, 1991)

M Argyle, *Psychology and Religion* (Routledge, 2000)

M Argyle, *The Psychological Perspective on Religious Experience* (RERU, 1997)

Augustine, *Confessions* (Penguin, 1961)

P Badham, *Religious and Near-Death Experience in Relation to Belief in a Future Life* (RERC, 1997)

C Batson, *Religion and the Individual* (OUP, 1993)

F Bauerschmidt, *Why the Mystics Matter Now* (Sorin, 2003)

B Beit-Hallahmi and M Argyle, *The Psychology of Religious Behaviour, Belief and Experience* (Routledge, 1997)

S Blackmore, *Journal of Near Death Studies* (1989)

G Claridge, *Origins of Mental Illness* (Blackwell, 1985)

D Cohn-Sherbok, *Jewish and Christian Mysticism* (Continuum, 1994)

P Cole, *Philosophy of Religion*, 2nd edition (Hodder, 2004)

S Davis, *God, Reason and Theistic Proofs* (Edinburgh University Press, 2000)

R Dawkins, *A Devil's Chaplain* (Weidenfeld & Nicolson, 2003)

R Dawkins, *The Blind Watchmaker* (Penguin, 1986)

P Donovan, *Interpreting Religious Experience* (Sheldon, 1979)

M Eliade, *Mythologies of Death* (Pennsylvania University Press, 1977)

S Evans, *Thinking About Faith* (IVP, 1985)

N Everitt, *The Non-existence of God* (Routledge, 2004)

P Fenwick, *The Truth in the Light* (Hodder, 1995)

C Franks Davis, *The Evidential Force of Religious Experience* (Clarendon Press, 1989)

J Frazer, *The Golden Bough* (Penguin Classic, 1996)

R Geaves, *The Sufis of Britain* (Cardiff Academic Press, 2000)

B Graham, *World Aflame* (Doubleday, 1966)

AM Greeley, *Sociology of the Paranormal* (Sage, 1975)

C Green, *Out-of-the-Body Experiences* (Institute of Psychophysical Research, 1968)

FC Happold, *Mysticism: A Study and Anthology* (Penguin, 1963)

A Hardy, *The Spiritual Nature of Man* (Oxford, 1979)

J Harvey, *Religious Experience in Contemporary Society* (RERC, 1997)

D Hay, *Inner Space* (Oxford, 1987)

D Hay, *Religious Experience Today* (Mowbray, 1990)

J Hick, *God and the Universe of Faiths* (Oneworld, 1973)

RW Hood Jr and RJ Morris, *Journal for the Scientific Study of Religion*, 20 (1981)

M Jakobsen, *Negative Religious Experiences* (Alister Hardy Centre, 1999)

W James, *The Varieties of Religious Experience* (Collins, 1960 edition)

J Kildahl, *The Psychology of Speaking in Tongues* (Hodder, 1972)

A Kose, *Conversion to Islam* (Kegan Paul, 1996)

HD Lewis, *Our Experiences of God* (Collins, 1959)

HD Lewis, *The Self and Immortality* (Macmillan, 1973)

J Lofland and N Skonovd, *Journal for the Scientific Study of Religion*, 20 (1981)

K Lowney, *Baring Our Souls* (Aldine de Gruyter, 1999)

A McGrath, *Christian Spirituality* (Blackwell, 1999)

A McGrath, *Christian Theology: An Introduction* (Blackwell, 1994)

A McGrath, *Dawkins' God, Genes, Memes and the Meaning of Life* (Blackwell, 2004)

A McGrath, *Science and Religion* (Blackwell, 1999)

A McGrath, *The Twilight of Atheism* (Rider, 2004)

M McGuire, *Religion: The Social Context* (Wadsworth, 1997)

J Mackie, *The Miracle of Theism* (Oxford, 1982)

TR Miles, *Religious Experience* (Macmillan, 1972)

M Momen, *The Phenomenon of Religion* (Oneworld, 1999)

H Montefiore, *The Paranormal – A Bishop Investigates* (Upfront, 2002)

R Moody, *Life after Life* (Mockingbird, 1975)

R Moody, *Reflections of Life after Life* (Mockingbird, 1977)

R Nicholson, *The Mystics of Islam* (Routledge, 1914)

K Osis and E Haraldsson, *At the Hour of Death* (Avon, 1977)

R Otto, *The Idea of the Holy* (OUP, 1923, 2nd edition 1950)

W Pahnke, The psychedelic mystical experience in the human encounter with death. *Psychedelic Review*, Number 11 (1971)

W Paley, *Natural Theology* (Ibis, reprint 1986)

M Palmer, *The Question of God* (Routledge, 2001)

W Penfield, *The Mystery of the Mind* (Princeton University Press, 1975)

M Persinger, *Neuropsychological Bases of God Beliefs* (Praeger, 1987)

M Peterson, *Contemporary Debates in Philosophy of Religion* (Blackwell, 2004)

JB Phillips, *Ring of Truth* (Hodder, 1967)

A Pierson, *George Muller of Bristol* (Pickering, 1899)

M Poloma, *The Toronto Report* (Terra Nova, 1996)

M Poloma and Gallup, *The Varieties of Prayer: A Survey Report* (Trinity, 1991)

VS Ramachandran, *Phantoms in the Brain* (Fourth Estate, 1998)

St Teresa, *The Collected Works of St Teresa of Avila* (ICS Publications, 1987)

R Siegel, The psychology of life after death. *American Psychologist*, 35 (1980)

N Smart, *Philosophers and Religious Truth* (SCM, 1964)

N Smart, *The Religious Experience of Mankind* (Fontana, 1969)

M Smith, *The Way of the Mystics* (Sheldon, 1976)

J Spickard, Experiencing religious rituals. *Sociological Analysis*, 52 (1991)

W Stace, *Mysticism and Philosophy* (Macmillan, 1960)

R Stannard, *The God Experiment* (Faber, 1999)

R Swinburne, *Is there a God?* (OUP, 1996)

R Swinburne, *The Existence of God* (OUP, 1979)

M Taylor, *Critical Terms for Religious Studies* (University of Chicago, 1998)

W Teasdall, *The Mystic Heart* (New World, 1999)

T Tennent, *Christianity at the Religious Roundtable* (Baker, 2002)

A Thiselton, *A Concise Encyclopedia of the Philosophy of Religion* (Oneworld, 2002)

P Tillich, *Systematic Theology* (Nisbet & Co., 1951)

G Uhlein, *Meditations with Hildegard of Bingen* (Bear & Co., 1983)

W Wainwright, *Philosophy of Religion* (Wadsworth, 1988)

G Wakefield, *Groundwork of Christian Spirituality* (Epworth, 2001)

K Ward, *Religion and Human Nature* (Clarendon, 1998)

J Webber, *Revelation and Religious Experience* (Abacus, 1995)

B Wilson, *Religious Experience: A Sociological Perspective* (RERU, 1996)

D Wulff, *Psychology of Religion* (Wiley & Sons, 1991)

R Zaehner, *Hindu and Muslim Mysticism* (Oneworld, 1994)

R Zaehner, *Mysticism: Sacred and Profane* (Clarendon, 1957)

C Zaleski, *Otherworld Journeys* (OUP, 1987)

# Index